FABLES AND PROVERBS

FABLES AND PROVERBS

from the Sanskrit

BEING THE

HITOPADESA

TRANSLATED BY

CHARLES WILKINS

WITH AN INTRODUCTION BY HENRY MORLEY

GYAN

Published by

GYAN

Gyan Publishing House
5, Ansari Road
Daryaganj, New Delhi-110002
Phone: 011-47034999, 9811692060
E-mail: books@gyanbooks.com

Distribution Network
gyanbooks.com
India, USA, Canada, UK, Australia, France

ISBN : 978-81-212-9630-4 (PB)
First Published, 1885

2nd Impression 2023

Printed at: Gyan Press, Delhi.

FABLES AND PROVERBS
Translated by: CHARLES WILKINS

FABLES AND PROVERBS

From the Sanskrit

BEING THE

HITOPADESA

TRANSLATED BY

CHARLES WILKINS

WITH AN INTRODUCTION BY HENRY MORLEY

LL.D., LATE PROFESSOR OF ENGLISH LITERATURE AT
UNIVERSITY COLLEGE, LONDON

INTRODUCTION.

In the family of languages to which English belongs, the Indo-European Family, Sanskrit is eldest brother. The parent language was spoken in a remote prehistoric time by a people living somewhere about the five rivers of the Punjaub. By migrations of that people westward there were afterwards established all the nations of the Iranian, Slavonic, Celtic, Teutonic and Classical stocks. The parent language, Aryan, has itself long since been lost; but its words, subjected to regular varieties of change, have passed into many lands. Additions have been many, but those words of which the roots are common to us all, bear witness to the common origin of the chief nations of Europe, and to their brotherhood with races now in India.

Descendants of that remote prehistoric Aryan people, who remained in India and were less remote, but also prehistoric, spoke Sanskrit. They left in their own tongue sacred books by which Sanskrit was established as a classical language. It was cultivated by the religious orders and used as the language in which all high religious teaching was enshrined. Thus its grammar was studied and preserved, and the language itself, first born of the old Aryan, has been maintained in its purity until this day. As the vernacular speech of a living people, applied to all their common daily wants, Sanskrit has not been used within the memory of man, but in some parts of India the vernacular does not differ from it very greatly.

The oldest Sanskrit books are at the fountain-head of European literature. These are the four Vedas, regarded as the source of all other Sastras or sacred books. The Vedas are written in an Iambic measure of eight syllables, and the earliest of them have been assigned by Sir William Jones to a date as early as 1500 years before Christ. The word Veda means knowledge, but though names of authors of the several parts were preserved, the whole was taken to mean inspired knowledge, "the self-evident word proceeding out of the mouth of God, this is the Veda." The first of the Vedas, called Rig from a word meaning praise, expresses the relations b tween man and God. The second, called Yajur, from a word meaning worship, contains instructions upon ceremonial. The third, called Sama, from a word signifying a prayer arranged for singing, contains pieces arranged as chants. Atharva, the fourth Veda, less ancient than the rest, contains forms of imprecation, prayers, hymns, and fifty-two theological treatises called Upanishads. Atharvan is referred to in it as a king appointed by Brahma to protect inferior beings. There are also detached Upanishads which are regarded as of less authority than the fifty-two contained in the Atharva-Veda. The Upanishads, or argumentative parts of the Vedas, are regarded as forming the Jnána, or philosophical part of the sacred books, and theological argument is based on these; the parts devoted to pure teaching of the religious system, its customs, sacrifices, ceremonies, form the Brahmanas; and the prayers and hymns in each Veda constitute its Sanhita. Thus, with regard to this matter the Vedas are said to contain Brahmanas, Jnána and Sanhita. The Brahmanas recognize a three-fold Veda, not reckoning the fourth, and derive the third from the first, the Rig-Veda, which teaches that there is one only supreme God, a pure spirit dwelling in eternal rest and silence, who is All, and in All. He is the supreme Brahma, who created the world by three manifestations drawn from himself, and named Brahmá, Vishnu, Siva, originally united in one essence, so that "the great One" became known as one Person and three gods. Brahmá represents Creation, Vishnu Preservation, and Siva Destruction. Of Vishnu, the Preserver, there have been nine Avatars or Incarnations, the first six were in the golden age of the world, the seventh was as Rama, the eighth as Krishna, the ninth as Buddha. The tenth, in which he will appear as a white horse, is yet awaited. In his last Avatar, as Buddha, Vishnu promoted scepticism to the end that the giants, wanting faith, might cease to obtain by prayer the powers that they misapplied.

The time during which the Vedas were produced extended over centuries, with periodic changes of style, and has been divided into four periods, the last of which, from 600 to 200 B.C., was the period of Sutra literature. Sutra means a string, and stands for a literature of short sayings strung together, by teachers who studied brevity, and of whom it was said, in their own proverbial way, that an author rejoiceth in the economizing of half a short vowel as much as in the birth of a son.

There were drawn from the four Vedas four Upa-Vedas. One was on Medicine from the Rig-Veda; one on Music from the Sáma-Veda; one on Arms and Implements of War, from the Yajur-Veda; and one on sixty-four Mechanical Arts, from the Atharva-Veda. The Upa-Vedas are now lost.

Also there were six Vedangas, or limbs of the Veda, treating severally of six sciences needed for interpretation of the sacred books. They were Pronunciation, Grammar, Prosody, Explanation of difficult words or phrases, Religious Ceremonial, and Astrology. To these were added four Upangas or additional limbs; History (the Purana): Logic (the Nyaya); Moral Philosophy (the Mimansa); and Jurisprudence (the Dharma-Sastra).

The earliest of these sacred writings, in their earliest period, were preserved only by oral tradition. They continued to live in the persons of men of the sacred caste, and thus different texts or versions of the Vedas, known as Sakhas, were preserved in different Charanas or schools of the Brahmans, who preserved the books in memory. A name for a Brahman settlement was a Parishad. It was said that "four or even three able men from among the Brahmans in a village who know the Veda and keep the sacrificial fire, form a Parishad." Members of different Parishads might be associated in one school or Charana.

Of the Law Books, or Dharma-Sastras, the most ancient and most famous is that known as the "Institutes of Manu," first translated into English by Sir William Jones. Manu was fabled to be the son of Brahmá, to have preserved the Vedas from destruction in the Hindoo deluge, and to have given in that Book of Laws an abstract of their contents.

The Indians had also six Darsanas, or systems of philosophy, all seeking the highest good in eternal happiness, and all accepting the authority of the Vedas but interpreting them variously. The six systems are essentially three. One, the Nyaya, brings knowledge in through the five channels of the senses; one, the Sankhya, looks to the emotions, and seeks the sources of pleasure, pain, and the neutral state of indifference, in which states alone it holds external nature to consist; one, the Vedantin, seeks only to determine what Is or Is Not. Besides the philosophy of the Darsanas, there were the teachings of several sects; among which the most important in their influence on thought was that of the Buddhists, chief opponents of the Brahmans. Their founder, Buddha Sakya Muni, began his teaching at an uncertain date, but it prevailed in India and Ceylon in the third century before Christ, and was introduced into China A.D. 61. Though the Brahmans finally prevailed in India, the Buddhists held their own in Ceylon, Burmah and China. They denied the existence of the One First Cause represented by the Brahma who gave forth Brahmá, Vishnu and Siva to create, preserve, destroy; One who is All in All, and of whom all forms of divinity—Indra, the Heavens with his thunderbolt and thousand eyes; Surya, the sun; Agni, fire; Pavana, wind; Varuna, ocean—are manifestations Not less were the elements of human life and death such manifestations of the God in all,—Ganasa, wisdom, perfecter of work; Lakshmi, goddess of prosperity, formed by the churning of the sea; Saraswati, goddess of learning; and Yama, judge of the dead.

Epic and dramatic poetry form also a part of Sanskrit literature. The two great Sanskrit epics are the Ramáyana, or Adventures of Rama (one of the incarnations of Vishnu), and the Maha-bhárata; both of them less ancient than the Vedas, but both so old that, like the Vedas, they were long preserved by oral tradition before they were committed to writing. The Maha-bhárata is in eighteen books, containing altogether 220,000 lines, and is a collection of national legends. In old Indian legend there were two dynasties of the north; those of the Sun, those of the Moon. Rama, the hero of the Ramáyana, was of the line of the Sun; Bhárata, the hero of the chief story in the Maha-bhárata, was of the line of the Moon.

The Bhagavad-Gita is an episode in the Maha-bhárata, a divine song in the form of a calm dialogue on eighteen subjects held between Krishna, the eighth Avatar of Vishnu, and his pupil Arjuna, while tumult of battle raged around them.

The great dramatist in Sanskrit literature was Kalidasa, author of the Sakuntala. The oldest known collection of Fables is the Pancha-Tantra, a collection into Five Tantras or sections, which is represented by the book now in the reader's hand, The Hitopadesa, or Friendly Instructor, in four books. The purpose of its interwoven fables and maxims was to present, in a way likely to win and keep attention, a system of good counsel for right training of a prince in all the chief affairs of life. It comes to us from a far place and time as a manual of worldly wisdom, inspired throughout by the religion of its place and time. There are, in fact, so far as concern the great forces of Nature, but accidental differences between the cities of men or the ant-hills of to-day and yesterday. When allowance has been made for some real progress in civilization, as in the recognition of the place of women in society, every fable in the Hitopadesa can still be applied to human character; every maxim quoted from the wise men of two or three thousand years ago, when parted from the local accidents of form, might find its time for being quoted now in church, at home, or upon 'Change.

H. M.

September, 1885.

TRANSLATOR'S PREFACE.

THE following translation, begun and completed this summer during a temporary residence at Bath, is a faithful portrait of a beautiful work, which in the opinions of many learned men, natives and Europeans, with whom I had the honour to converse upon the subject before I left Bengal, is the Sanskrit original of those celebrated fables, which after passing through most of the Oriental languages, ancient and modern, with various alterations to accommodate them to the taste and genius of those for whose benefit or amusement they were designed, and under different appellations, at length were introduced to the knowledge of the European world with a title importing them to have been originally written by Pilpay, or Bidpai, an ancient Brahman; two names of which, as far as my inquiries have extended, the Brahmans of the present times are totally ignorant. Sir William Jones, whose surprising talents are ever employed in seeking fresh sources of knowledge, and promoting their cultivation, in an elegant discourse delivered by him the 26th of February, 1786, since my return from India, at a meeting of the Society for inquiring into the History, civil and natural, the Antiquities, Arts, Sciences, and Literature of Asia, expresses his sentiments upon this subject in the following words :—

"Their (the Hindoos) Niti-Sastra, or System of Ethics, is yet preserved, and the fables of Vishnu-Serma, whom we ridiculously call Pilpay, are the most beautiful, if not the most ancient, collection of Apologues in the world. They were first translated from the Sanskrit in the sixth century, by Buzer-chumihr, or "bright as the sun," the chief physician, and afterwards the Vizier of the great Anushirwan, and are extant under various names in more than twenty languages. but their original title is Hitopadesa, or "amicable instruction ;" and as the very existence of Æsop, whom the Arabs believe to have been an Abyssinian, appears rather doubtful, I am not disinclined to suppose that the first moral fables which appeared in Europe were of Indian or Ethiopian origin."

Granting the Hitopadesa be the work it is supposed to be, to save the learned reader the trouble of referring to other books to trace its history, I have here brought all I have collected upon the subject under one view.

The learned Fraser, in his catalogue of Oriental manuscripts, under the article Ayar Danish, speaks thus: "The ancient Brahmins of India, after a great deal of time and labour, compiled a treatise (which they called Kurtuk Dumnik*) in which were inserted the choicest treasures of wisdom, and the perfectest rules for governing a people. This book they presented to their Rajahs, who kept it with the greatest secrecy and care. About the time of Mahommed's birth, or the latter end of the sixth century, Noishervan the Just, who then reigned in Persia, discovered a great inclination to see that book: for which purpose one Burzuvia, a physician, who had a surprising talent in learning several languages, particularly the Sanskrit, was introduced to him as the properest person to be employed to get a copy thereof. He went to India; where, after some years' stay, and great trouble, he procured it. It was translated into the Pehluvi language by him, and Buzrjumehr the Vizier. Noishervan ever after, and all his successors, the Persian kings, had this book in high esteem, and took the greatest care to keep it secret. At last Abu Jaffer Mansour zu Nikky, who was the second Khaliff of the Abassi reign, by great search got a copy thereof in the Pehluvi language, and ordered Iman Hossan Abdal Mokaffa, who was the most learned of the age, to translate it into Arabic. This prince ever after made it his guide,

* The Karattaka and Damanaka of the following work.

and not only in affairs relating to the government, but in private life also.

"In the year 380 of the Hegira, Sultan Mahmud Ghazi put it into verse. And afterwards, in the year 515, by order of Bheram Shah ben Massaud, that which Abdal Mokaffa had translated was retranslated into Persic, by Abul Mala Nasser Allah Mustofi; and this is that Kulila Dumna which is now extant. As this latter had too many Arabic verses and obsolete phrases in it, Molana Ali ben Hossein Vaez, at the request of Emir Soheli, keeper of the seals to Sultan Hossein Mirza, put it into a more modern style, and gave it the title of Anuar Soheli.

"In the year 1002, the Great Moghol Jalal o' Din Mahommed Akbar ordered his own secretary and vizier, the learned Abul Fazl, to illustrate the obscure passages, abridge the long digressions, and put it into such a style as would be most familiar to all capacities; which he accordingly did, and gave it the name of Ayar Danish, or the Criterion of Wisdom."

From other sources I have drawn the following conclusions:—That in the year 1709, the Kulila Dumna, the Persian version of Abul Mala Nasser Allah Mustofi made in the 515th year of the Hegira, was translated into French with the title of "Les Conseils et les Maximes de Pilpay, Philosophe Indien, sur les divers Etats de la Vie." This edition resembles the Hitopadesa more than any other I have seen, and is evidently the immediate original of the English "Instructive and entertaining Fables of Pilpay, an ancient Indian Philosopher," which in 1775 had gone through five editions.

The Anuar Soheli above mentioned, about the year 1540 was rendered into the Turkish language, and the translator is said to have bestowed twenty years' labour upon it. In the year 1724, this edition M. Galland began to translate into French, and the four first chapters were then published; but in the year 1778 M. Cardonne completed the work in three volumes, giving it the name of "Contes et Fables Indiennes de Bidpai et de Lokman; traduites d'Ali Tchelebi-ben Saleh auteur Turk."

If the Hitopadesa of Vishnu-Serma be, as we have every reason to conclude, the prototype of the several compositions which have been mentioned, its age is tolerably ascertained to be upwards of eleven hundred years. Few Sanskrit books bear either the name of the real author or the date of the year in which they were written; and it is to circumstantial evidence we must generally trust for the proof of either.

In executing this work I have scrupulously adhered to the text; and I have preferred drawing a picture of which it may be said—"I can suppose it a strong likeness, although I am unacquainted with the original," to a flattering portrait, where characteristic features, because not altogether consonant to European taste, must have been sacrificed to the harmony of composition.

CHARLES WILKINS.

QUEEN'S SQUARE, BLOOMSBURY,
1st *November*, 1787.

CONTENTS.

CHAPTER III.

OF DISPUTING.

CHAPTER IV.

OF MAKING PEACE.

THE HITOPADESA:

FABLES AND PROVERBS.

AUTHOR'S INTRODUCTION.

Reverence to Ganes! *

Reverence to Saraswatee! †

'MAY the completion, through the mercy of Dhoorjatee,‡ on whose head is planted a crescent among the frothy streams of Janhavee,§ be for the edification of the worthy!

* The god of prudence and policy.

† The goddess of harmony and the arts.

‡ One of the titles of Seeva, the Deity in his destroying quality. The word signifies, *he who weareth his hair bound about his head in the form of a tiara*, as it is now worn by those penitents who are known in India by the name of Yogees or Sanyasees.

§ A name of the river Ganga, or the Ganges, as it is erroneously called. This river is supposed to flow from the hair of Seeva. The truth seems to be, that Seeva is the name of the mountain in which is the source of that river; for amongst other epithets usually given to that Deity, is found that of Geereesa, *Lord of mountains;* and his consort is commonly called Doorga, a place of *difficult access*, and Parvatee, a patronymic formed from *parvata*, a mountain.

'This work, entitled Hitopadesa,* affordeth elegance in the Sanskrit † idioms, in every part variety of language, and inculcateth the doctrine of prudence and policy.

'The wise man should study the acquisition of science and riches, as if he were not subject to sickness and death; but to the duties of religion he should attend, as if death had seized him by the hair.

'Knowledge produceth humility; from humility proceedeth worthiness; from worthiness riches are acquired; from riches religion,‡ and thence happiness.

'Of all things knowledge is esteemed the most precious treasure; because of its incapacity to be stolen, to be given away, or ever to be consumed.

'Knowledge introduceth a man to acquaintance; and, as the humble stream to the ocean, so doth it conduct him into the hard-acquired presence of the prince, whence fortune floweth.

* A compound of *hita*, health, welfare, *upa*, a preposition, implying *proximity*, and *desa* signifying a *showing* or *pointing*. The common acceptation of the word is *useful*, or *beneficial*, *instruction*.

† The learned language of the Brahmans is so called. It is a compound of *san* (the *m* of *sam* being, by rule, changed to *n*, before a dental *s*; as the *m* of the Latin *com* before the same letter in the word *construction*), a preposition signifying *completion*, and *skrita* (for *krita*), *done*, *made*, *finished*.

‡ According to our mode of thinking this seems odd; but where religion consists in sacrifices, and other expensive ceremonies, a poor man hath but a sad chance of providing for his future happiness.

'There are two species of knowledge in use: the knowledge of arms, and the knowledge of books. The first is the scoff of the wise, whilst the last is for ever honoured.

'As the impressions made upon a new vessel are not easily to be effaced, so here youth are taught prudence through the allurement of fable.'

This work is divided under four heads:—The Acquisition of a Friend. The Separation of a Favourite. Of Disputing. Of making Peace. And it is, chiefly, drawn and written from the Tantra and other Sastras.*

On the banks of the river Bhageeratheet† there is a remarkable city called Pataneeputra,‡ where there was formerly a Rajah, endued with every noble quality, whose name was Sudarsana.§ One day he heard the two following verses, as they were repeating by some one:

* The translator has reason to suppose that these words extend only to the maxims, which are, in the original, in verse, and are known to be quotations from other authors; particularly from the Mahabharat, the Smreetee-sastra of Manoo, the Geeta, and, as the author himself says, the Tantra-sastra.

† The river Ganges.

‡ An ancient name for the city which is now called Patna.

§ All the proper names throughout this work are, like this, significant. They have an awkward appearance when translated, which is the reason so few have been rendered into English. The names of persons in India are, to this day, all significant, and, for the most part, derived from the Sanskrit.

'He who is not possessed of such a book as will dispel many doubts, point out hidden treasures, and is, as it were, a mirror of all things, is even an ignorant man.

'Youth, abundant wealth, high birth, and inexperience, are, each of them, the source of ruin. What then must be the fate of him in whom all four are combined?'

The Rajah had no sooner heard these lines than he began to consider, with an afflicted heart, the situation of his sons, who were yet unacquainted with books, and wandering in the paths of error.

'What benefit is there in a son who is neither learned nor virtuous! Or, of what use is a sightless eye? Such an eye is but pain!'

Again:

'He is truly born, by whose birth his generation is exalted; or else, who is there in this transitory life, who being dead, is not born again?' *

So it is said:

'Of the child unborn, the dead, and the fool, the two first, and not the last, are the least to be lamented; for the two first cause but a transient sorrow, whilst the last is an eternal plague.'

* The reader, in this and similar passages, will not fail to recollect that it is a Hindoo who speaks, fully persuaded of the metempsychosis.

Again:

'One child of genius is a blessing; not so even a hundred fools. A single moon dispelleth darkness better than a host of stars.

'The child of him, whose transgressions are expiated by penances performed at places of holy pilgrimage, should be obedient, prosperous, virtuous, and happy.'

And it is said also:

'An influx of riches, and constant health; a wife who is dear to one, and one who is of kind and gentle speech; a child who is obedient, and useful knowledge, are, my son, the six pleasures of life.

'A father who contracteth debts is an enemy, and a mother false to her bed; a beautiful wife is an enemy; an ignorant son is an enemy.

'Learning to the inexperienced is a poison; eating upon a full stomach is a poison; the society of the vulgar is a poison; a young wife to an old man is a poison.

'A man is respected, even for the merits of his son. Let the cane* of the bow be ever so clean, deficient in other qualities, what will it do?'

* In the original the word which is translated *cane* (vangs) signifies, not only a *bamboo*, of which they make their bows, but also a *race* or *family*. The Hindoo authors are but too apt to play upon words, and are always happy to apply a term that has two meanings diametrically opposite, which is, very often, exceedingly perplexing to a translator.

Alas! my son, that so many nights have sweetly passed away, and thou art still untaught; wherefore, in the society of the learned, thou sinkest like an ox in the mire.

Then how shall these my sons be now rendered accomplished? when it is said,

'The age, the actions, the wealth, the knowledge, and even the death, of every one is determined in his mother's womb.

'The determined fate of all beings, let them be ever so great, inevitably happeneth. Nakedness is the fate of Neelakant,* and of Hari† sleeping on a great serpent.

'What is not to be, that is not to be; if it be to

* One of the titles of Seeva.

† Hari is one of the titles of Vishnu, the Deity in his preserving quality. Nearly opposite Sultan-gunge, a considerable town in the province of Bahar in the East Indies, there stands a rock of granite, forming a small island in the midst of the Ganges, known to Europeans by the name of *the rock of Jehangueery*, which is highly worthy of the traveller's notice for a vast number of images carved in relief upon every part of its surface. Amongst the rest there is Hari, of a gigantic size, recumbent upon a coiled serpent, whose heads, which are numerous, the artist has contrived to spread into a kind of canopy over the sleeping god; and from each of its mouths issues a forked tongue, seeming to threaten instant death to any whom rashness might prompt to disturb him. The whole figure lies almost clear of the block on which it is hewn. It is finely imagined, and executed with great skill. The Hindoos are taught to believe, that at the end of every *kalpa* (creation or formation), all things are absorbed in the Deity, and that in the interval of another creation he reposeth himself upon the serpent *sesha* (duration), who is also called *ananta* (endless). The allegory is too plain to require any further explanation.

come to pass, it cannot be otherwise. This reasoning is an antidote. Why doth not the afflicted drink of it?'

But such are the idle sentiments of certain men who admit not of works; for,

'Whilst a man confideth in providence, he should not slacken his own exertions; for without labour he is unworthy to obtain the oil from the seed.

'Fortune attendeth that lion amongst men who exerteth himself. They are weak men who declare fate the sole cause.

'Subdue fate, and exert human strength to the utmost of your power; and if, when pains have been taken, success attend not, in whom is the blame?

'As the chariot will not move upon a single wheel; even so fate succeedeth not without human exertion.

'It is said, fate is nothing but the deeds committed in a former state of existence; wherefore, it behoveth a man vigilantly to exert the powers he is possessed of.*

'As the potter formeth the lump of clay into what-

* To enable the reader to comprehend this verse, and many similar passages, it is necessary to inform him that many of the Hindoos believe this to be a place of rewards and punishments, as well as of probation. Thus good and bad luck are the fruit of good and evil deeds committed in a former life. To prevent the latter in a future life, *it behoveth a man*, &c.

ever shape he liketh, even so may a man regulate his own actions.'*

Again:

'Although, in the story of the crow and tal† fruit, one was seen to have found a treasure before him, fate of itself did not present it: some exertion was still expected.

'Good fortune is the offspring of our endeavours, although there be nothing sweeter than ease. The deer are not wont to precipitate themselves into the mouth of the sleeping lion.

'The boy who hath been exercised under his parents' care, attaineth the state of an accomplished man; but the child becometh not a Pandit whilst in the state he dropped from the womb.

'That mother is an enemy, and that father a foe, by whom not having been instructed, their son shineth not in the assembly; but appeareth there, like a booby among geese.‡

* This verse is connected with that which precedes it, and seems to imply, that we have it in our power to secure prosperity in a future birth.

† The translator never saw the story alluded to. Probably it is some fable, where a foolish crow expected the fruit here mentioned, and which is that of the fan palmira, should come to him, rather than that he who saw it at a distance, should exert himself to possess it.

‡ The bird here called *a booby* (in the original *vaka*), is of the stork species, and the emblem of stupidity, as *the goose* is of eloquence and elegance, amongst the Hindoo poets. Saraswati, their goddess of Harmony, has her goose, as Minerva her owl.

'Men deficient in learning shine not, although they may be possessed of youth and beauty, and of a noble race. They are like the flower Kinsuk, destitute of fragrance.

'A fool, too, may shine in the assembly, dressed in fine garments; but the fool shineth no longer than he holdeth his tongue.'

The Rajah having thus meditated for a while, convened a council of Pandits, whom he addressed in the following words:—"Ye learned men, attend! Is there a man to be found who shall, by precepts drawn from Neeti-Sastras,* be able to perfect the birth of my sons, who are yet uninformed, and constantly wandering in the paths of error? For,

'As a piece of glass, from the vicinity of gold, acquireth the colour of a topaz; so a fool may derive some consequence from the presence of a wise man.'

Again:

'The mind is depraved by the society of the low; it riseth to equality with equals; and to distinction with the distinguished.'"

Of this assembly there was a great Pandit by name Vishnu-Sarma,† well versed in the principles of all

* Systems of morality and policy.

† Pandit is an honorary title given to learned Brahmans. A doctor of the Hindoo laws. A Hindoo philosopher. It is not easy to determine whether Vishnu-Sarma was really the author, or only the com-

the Neeti-Sastras, as it were another Vrihaspati,* who replied :—"These young princes, O mighty Rajah! being the offsprings of an illustrious race, are capable of being instructed in the Neeti-Sastras ; but

'Labour, bestowed on nothing, is fruitless : with infinite pains a booby will not, presently, talk like a parrot.

'In a noble race, levity without virtue is seldom found. In a mine of rubies, when shall we find pieces of glass?'

Wherefore, I will engage, that in the space of six months, I will render thy sons well acquainted with the doctrines of the Neeti-Sastras."

The Rajah then respectfully said :

"Even a reptile, when attached to a flower, may mount upon the head of the holy ; even a stone, when set up and consecrated by the great, attaineth divinity.

For it is said,

'As a thing on the eastern mountains shineth by the presence of the sun ; so one of humble birth, even, may be enlightened by the allurements of good books.

piler of these fables ; but it is worthy of observation that the Brahmans themselves know nothiug of Pilpay, to whom, we are told, the Persians attribute them.

* The preceptor of the good spirits, and the planet Jupiter.

'Men of good or evil birth may be possessed of good qualities; but, falling into bad company, they become vicious. Rivers flow with sweet waters; but, having joined the ocean, they become undrinkable.'

Then be thou an example to these, my sons, for the acquisition of virtue." Having said this, he respectfully delivered his sons into the charge of Vishnu-Sarma; and that learned Pandit, soon after, seized the opportunity, when they were, for amusement, sitting together upon the terrace of their father's palace, to introduce his advice to the young princes in the following lines:

'Learning to a man is a name superior to beauty; learning is better than hidden treasure. Learning is a companion on a journey to a strange country; learning is strength inexhaustible. Learning is the source of renown, and the fountain of victory in the senate. Learning is a superior sight; learning is a livelihood; and a man in this world without learning is as a beast of the field.

'A country deprived of the Ganges is smitten; a family without learning is smitten; a woman without a child is smitten; a sacrifice without the Brahman's rights is smitten.

'Wise men pass their time in amusements drawn

from the works of the poets; whilst fools squander theirs in useless pursuits, sloth, or riot.'

"For your amusement, therefore," said he, "I am going to relate some curious stories of a crow, a tortoise, and other animals.'"

CHAPTER I.

THE ACQUISITION OF A FRIEND.

VISHNU-SARMA then told the young princes to attend, and said,—The present subject to be discussed is, "The Acquisition of a Friend;" to which these following lines are an introduction:

Wise and sincere friends, although poor and destitute of implements, may speedily effect our purposes; as in the instances of the crow, the tortoise, the deer, and the mouse.

The young princes demanded how this was; and Vishnu-Sarma related as follows:

FABLE I.

ON the banks of the river Godavaree there was a Salmalee* tree, to whose spreading branches birds of various species were wont to flock from every quarter, to roost. Early one morning, when darkness was dispersing, and the moon, whose emblem is the flower Kumudini-nayaka,† was reclining upon the summit

* The silk cotton tree, commonly called *seemal*.

† A species of lotus which blossoms only in the night.

of the mountain Charama, a certain crow, whose name was Laghupatanaka,* being awake, chanced to espy a fowler coming that way, who appeared to him an another angel of death. Having regarded him, and considered for a moment, he said to himself,—This unwelcome visit happeneth to day very early, and I know not what may be the consequence. So, pondering upon what he saw, he was seized with a panic, and flew out of the way; for,

'A thousand occasions for sorrow, and a hundred for fear, day by day assail the fool; not so the wise man.'

Yet it is said that men of the world must absolutely act according to these lines:

'Every time we rise, great fear is to be apprehended; for, to-day, of death, sickness, and sorrow, who knoweth which may fall upon us?'

The fowler, having first strewed some rice upon the ground, spread his nets; and whilst this was transacting, it happened that Chitra-greeva,† the chief of a flock of pigeons, was in the air flying about with his attendants. He saw the grains of rice upon the ground; and perceiving that his flock showed an inclination to partake of them, he addressed them thus:—Beware, my friends! Whence, think you,

* Light-flier. † Motley-neck.

should rice be produced in a place like this, void of inhabitants? Let this, therefore, be investigated; for I conceive no good can come of it, lest we should experience a fate similar to what is mentioned in the following lines:

A traveller, through lust of gold, being plunged into an inextricable mire, is killed and devoured by an old tiger.

How did this happen? demanded the pigeons, and their chief related as follows:

FABLE II.

As I was travelling on the southern road, once upon a time, I saw an old tiger seated upon the bank of a large river, with a bunch of kusa* grass in his paw, calling out to every one who passed,—Ho! ho! traveller, take this golden bracelet. But every one was afraid to approach him to receive it. At length, however, a certain traveller, tempted by avarice, regarded it as an instance of good fortune; but, said he, in this there is personal danger, in which we are not warranted to proceed.

'Confidence should not be put in rivers; in

* A species of grass esteemed sacred by the Brahmans, and used in most of their religious ceremonies. The lion in this fable is made to hold it in his paw, to appear like a devotee, and to beget confidence.

animals which have claws or horns; in men with weapons in their hands ; nor in women ; nor in those of royal birth.

'It is not good to pass by that we dislike, even to gain that which we like; for the water of life becometh mortal when mixed with a poison.'

Yet, said he, there is risk in every undertaking, for the acquisition of wealth. Hence, it is said,

'No man beholdeth prosperity who doth not encounter danger; but having encountered danger, if he surviveth, he beholdeth it.'

This I have considered, and now let me ask thee plainly, where is thy gold ? But stop, tigers eat men, and the opinion of the world is hard to be defeated ; for,

'The people, mere followers of one another, hold up a Brahman who is a cow-killer, as example in our religion.' *

I too, replied the tiger, have read religious books. Hear what they say,

'In granting and in refusing, in joy and in sorrow, in liking and in disliking, good men, because of their own likeness, show mercy unto all things which have life.

* This sentence undoubtedly alludes to some vulgar facts at the time well understood.

'As their own lives are most dear to them, so also are those of all creatures. Good men, because of their own likeness, show mercy unto all things which have life.

'A man, because of his own likeness, should learn this saying :—As rain to the parched field, so is meat to one oppressed with hunger.

'Charity is to be given to the poor, and is fruitful. O joy of the house of Pandu.' *

The traveller then asked him, where was the bracelet; and the tiger having held out his paw, showed it to him and said,—Look at it, it is a golden bracelet. How shall I place confidence in thee? said the traveller; and the tiger replied,—Formerly, in the days of my youth, I was of a very wicked disposition, and as a punishment for the many men and cattle I had murdered, my numerous children died, and I was also deprived of my wife; so, at present, I am destitute of relations. This being the case, I was advised, by a certain religious person, to practise charity and other religious duties; I am now grown extremely devout. I perform ablutions regularly, and am charitable. Why then am I not worthy of confidence?

* This hemistich, and the preceding three verses, seem to belong to the Mahabharata, and to be addressed to Arjoon, one of the five sons of Pandu.

'The study of what is ordained,* charity, mortifications of the flesh, and sacrifices; fortitude, forgiveness, rectitude, and modesty, form the true way, and are recorded the eightfold division of our duty.

'Of these, the first class, consisting of four, is attended to for the sake of hereafter; and the latter class of four, presideth in every great mind.'

So far, you see, continued the tiger, I have an interest in wishing to give away, to some one, this golden bracelet from off my own wrist; and as thou appearest to be rather a poor man, I prefer giving it to thee; according to this saying:

'Make choice of the poor, O son of Kuntee,† and bestow not thy gifts on others. Medicine is to be administered to the sick; for of what benefit is physic to those who are in health?'

And thus:

'The gift which is to be given, should be given gratuitously; in time, in place, and to a proper object; and such a gift is recorded a righteous gift.'

Then go, and having purified‡ thyself in this

* The study of the divine law.

† Kuntee is the name of the mother of three of the five sons of Paudu. Probably this address is to Arjoon, the youngest of those three.

‡ The Hindoos not only wash themselves after any impure action, but also before divine worship, and the receipt of any extraordinary benefit.

stream, take the golden bracelet.—The traveller no sooner begins to enter the river to purify himself, than he sticks fast in the mud, and is unable to escape. The tiger told him he would help him out; and creeping softly towards him, the poor traveller is seized, and instantly exclaims to himself,—Alas! the career of my heart is cut short by fate!

'The natural disposition of every animal conquereth, and presideth over his qualifications; for from that nature he passeth not, either for qualifications or ornamental accomplishments.

'He readeth not the Dharma-Sastra,*—is this the cause; or doth he not study the Vedas? † In this matter the natural disposition of his wicked spirit prevaileth, even as the milk of the cow is by nature sweet.‡

'What is done for those who have not their passions in subjection, is like washing the elephant.§ Service rendered to the unfortunate is, for the most part, like knowledge without practice.'

I did not well in that I placed confidence in one of such evil disposition; for it is said,

* Books containing men's moral and religious duties, as enjoined by the divine law.

† The word *ved*, or *veda*, signifies *knowledge* or *science*. The sacred writings of the Hindoos are so distinguished, of which there are four books.

‡ The greatest part of this verse, in the original, is so obliterated that the translator is by no means certain that he has given the meaning of his author.

§ Washing the blackamoor white.

'The natural, and no other qualities should be examined; for the natural qualities pass over all others, and mount upon the head.'

But whilst the unfortunate traveller was thus meditating on his fate, he was devoured by the tiger. I have said, therefore, "Through the lust of a bracelet," &c., and hence also, it is at no time proper to undertake anything without examination; as in the following saying:

'Well-digested food, a well-discerning child, a well-governed wife, a prince well served, a speech well considered, and an action well weighed, are not, even in very long time, attended by disagreeable consequences.'

One of the pigeons, who was of a haughty spirit, having heard what had been said, exclaimed,—Ha! what is this? Is it not said,

'In times of necessity the words of the wise are worthy to be observed; by whose determination we may freely engage in all things, even in eating.*

'All things upon the face of the earth, our meat and our drink, bear cause of suspicion; then how is forbearance to be exercised, and life to be supported?'

Again it is said,

* There is nothing a Hindoo is so scrupulous about as his eating. Even the menial servants of Europeans, who are the very refuse of the people, would rather starve than eat or drink after their masters.

'These six—the peevish, the niggard, the dissatisfied, the passionate, the suspicious, and those who live upon others' means—are for ever unhappy.'

So having heard these words, the whole flock flew down upon the grain.

'Those, even, who possess very many Sastras, are learned in the Vedas, and are the dispellers of doubt, experience trouble, when their reason is blinded by avarice.

'From covetousness proceedeth ill-nature, and of ill-nature is born stubbornness; from stubbornness is created a delusion of reason,* and that delusion is the cause of sin.

'The birth of a golden deer is impossible; nevertheless Ram longed for the chase.† In times of misfortune, men's understandings even are sullied.'

At length they were all, in consequence of their covetousness, confined by the threads of the net; and they presently began to lay the blame upon him, by whose advice they had descended. So it is said,

'A man should not strive to precede his fellows;

* To this delusion of reason, which in the original is expressed by a single word (*moha*) some Hindoo philosophers attribute all natural images which are presented to the mind through the medium of the senses; for, say they, remove this veil of ignorance, and it will be found that *matter* is a mere phantom.

† This passage seems to relate to some adventure in the wars of Ram against Ravan, the tyrant of Ceylon, which are the subject of a beautiful poem, called the "Ramayana."

for, should the work succeed, the booty is equal, and if it fail, the leader is punished.'

Chitra-greeva hearing their reproaches, said, It is not his fault. It is said,

'To those who are fallen into misfortunes, what was a blessing becometh an evil: to a child in confinement, its mother's knee is a binding post.

'He who hath the resolution to extricate one from his misfortunes, who is fallen into difficulties by another's fault, is a Pandit; not he who hesitateth about the means he should employ for the deliverance of the distressed.'

Hesitation, in times of misfortune, is the mark of a coward; wherefore, depend upon resolution, and let a remedy be thought of; according to these lines:

'Fortitude in adversity, and moderation in prosperity; eloquence in the senate, and courage in the field; great glory in renown, and labour in study; are the natural perfections of great minds.'

Again:

'There are here six faults, which a man ought to avoid: The desire of riches, drowsiness, sloth, idleness, tediousness, fear, and anger.'

Let this be done immediately: Let us all, with one accord, take up the net and fly away with it; according to these lines;

'Combination is best for men, either with their own tribe or with strangers; for even a grain of rice groweth not when divided from its husk.

'A combination even of small things serveth an occasion. An intoxicated elephant may be bound with a few straws, when formed into a rope.'

Having considered this, the pigeons, with one accord, took up the net, and flew away with it. Presently the fowler, seeing the robbers of his net at a great distance, pursued them; and, as he ran, these were his thoughts:

'These travellers of the air have combined to rob me of my net; but when they shall fall down, they will come into my power.'

But soon finding they had passed the confines of his sight, the poor fowler turned back from the pursuit.

The pigeons now demanded what was to be done; and Chitra-greeva replied,

'A mother is a friend, and a father is a friend; but both these are from nature kind; but there are others who are benevolent from casual motives.'

Our friend Hiranyaka,* the noble mouse, lives upon the banks of the Gandakee.† He may be able to gnaw our snare asunder with his teeth. Having con-

* Wealthy.

† A river which empties itself into the Ganges near Patna.

sidered this proposal, they all flew to the residence of Hiranyaka, who, from his constant dread of the crows, had made himself a hole with a hundred outlets, wherein he remained secured, according to this verse:

'There was an old mouse, well read in the Neeti-Sastras, who, before the approach of danger, kept himself within a hole with a hundred doors.'

He was startled with fear at the descent of the pigeons, and stood silent; upon which Chitra-greeva called out,—Friend Hiranyaka! what, wilt thou not speak to us? And Hiranyaka, upon recollecting his voice, slipped out of his hole, and exclaimed,—O how happy I am, that my dear friend Chitra-greeva is arrived!

'There is not in life a man more happy than he who hath a friend to converse with, a friend to live with, and a friend to embrace.'

But when he saw that they were confined in a net, he stood amazed for a moment, and demanded what it meant. Chitra-greeva replied,—What else, my friend, can it be, but the effect of the evil committed in a prior existence? Seeing thou art endued with great wisdom, what was the use of thy question? For is it not said,

Whatsoever cometh to pass, either good or evil,

is the consequence of a man's own actions, and descendeth from the power of the Supreme Ruler.

'Sickness, sorrow, and distress; bonds and punishment to corporeal beings, are fruit of the tree of of their own transgressions.'

Hiranyaka having heard these words, quickly ran to gnaw asunder the cords by which Chitra-greeva was confined. Not so, my friend, said Chitra-greeva, until thou hast cut asunder the bonds of these who are under my protection. Hiranyaka then said, I am weak, my friend, and my teeth are but delicate; how then am I able to bite open the snares which entangle them? As long as my teeth shall not break, so long will I gnaw thy snares; and afterwards, if it should be in my power, I will divide the cords which confine the rest. Let it be as I say, replied Chitra-greeva; and to the utmost of thy power try to subdue their bonds first.

Those, said the mouse, who are acquainted with the rules of prudence, do not approve, that for the preservation of those who are under our protection, we should abandon ourselves.

'A man should keep his riches against accidents, and with his riches he should save his family; but he should, on all occasions, save himself, both with his family and his riches.

'Our lives are for the purposes of religion, labour,

love, and salvation.* If these are destroyed, what is not lost? If these are preserved, what is not preserved?'

This may be so, replied Chitra-greeva; but I am not, by any means, able to suffer the afflictions of those who are here under my protection.

'A wise man should relinquish both his wealth and his life for another. All is to be surrendered for a just man, when he is reduced to the brink of destruction.'

Here is another unparalleled argument:

'In birth, substance, and quality, they are like unto me; say then, what will ever be the fruit of my superiority?'

Again:

'Without misfortune, they will not forsake me; then I will protect these who have taken sanctuary with me, even with the loss of my life.

'Why dost thou hesitate over this perishable body composed of flesh, bone, and excrements? O my friend, support my reputation!'

Another:

'If constancy is to be obtained by inconstancy,

* Union with the universal spirit of God, and a final exemption from mortal birth.

purity by impurity, reputation by the body, then, what is there which may not be obtained?

'The difference between the body and the qualities is infinite. The body is a thing to be destroyed in a moment, whilst the qualities * endure to the end of the creation.'

Hiranyaka having been attentive to what had been spoken, and being exceedingly pleased, exclaimed,—Nobly! nobly! my friend. By such generosity to those who are under thy protection, thou art worthy to be elevated to the supreme command over the regions of the three worlds.† Having said this, Hiranyaka gnawed asunder their bonds; and when he had addressed himself to all in respectful compliments of congratulation, he said,—Friend Chitra-greeva, always when you see a net, suspect great harm will come of it; and learn not to think meanly of yourself. But, alas!

'A bird who seeth her prey before her, even at the distance of a hundred yojan,‡ perceiveth not, if her time be come, the snares which are laid to entrap her.

* The Hindoos believe organized matter to be governed by three principles, which they term *satwa*, *raja*, and *tama*. The first inspires *truth*, the second *passion*, and the third *sin*.

† Celestial, terrestrial, and infernal regions.

‡ A land measure of about eight English miles.

'When I behold in eclipses * the distress of the moon and the author of day; elephants and serpents in confinement, and the worthy in indigence; alas! in my mind, destiny is all-powerful.

'Birds meet their fate whilst sporting in the air, and fishes, by artful means, are destroyed from the bottomless waters of the ocean.

'When laws are ill-enforced, where are their good morals? To whom is the mere glare of the fire a virtue? *Time* † is trouble, and the author of destruction; he seizeth even from afar.'

The mouse having taught this, and performed the duties of hospitality, Chitra-greeva took his leave, and with his flock departed for that country his inclination led him to; and Hiranyaka retired into his hole.

The crow, Laghu-patanaka, having been a spectator of all which had passed, now presently appeared and called out—What ho! Hiranyaka! Thou art worthy to be praised, to be adored, and to be a place of refuge, throughout the three regions of the world!

'Behold how many pigeons, his friends, even hundreds, have been delivered by the friendship of a mouse!'

In consequence of this, I too am anxious to form a

* The vulgar opinion of the Hindoos is, that these phenomena are produced by a large serpent, or dragon, seizing the sun and moon.

† Time is constantly personified by the Hindoo poets, and made the universal agent of death and destruction.

friendly acquaintance with thee. Then favour me with thy friendship. Hiranyaka having heard him, called out from the inside of his hole,—Who art thou? and he replied, I am a crow, and my name is Laghu-patanaka. Hiranyaka, upon hearing who he was, laughing said,—Having seen thy complexion, like broken anjan,* a beetle, a wild ox, a buffalo, or a woman's hair, what friendship can I have with thee?

'The wise man is united with that in this life with which it is proper he should be united. I am bread, thou art the eater. How then can harmony exist between us?'

As may be seen in a certain story, of which the following verse is the introduction:

Harmony between the food and the feeder is the forerunner of misfortune.—A deer, through the artifice of a jackal, is caught in a snare, but is preserved by a crow.

How did this happen? demanded Laghu-patanaka; and the mouse, Hiranyaka, related as follows:

FABLE III.

IN Magadha-desa † there is a forest called Champakavatee, and under the branches of one of the

* Crude antimony, and sometimes lead ore, of which they make a collyrium. These comparisons have a ridiculous appearance in English; but the Hindoos prefer the use of nonsense in their abuse, to curses and blasphemy.

† The country about the city of Gya was anciently so called.

champaka* trees there dwelt, in great good fellowship, a deer and a crow. One day, as the deer, who was plump and fat, was freely roaming about the woods, he was spied by a certain jackal, who having examined him, said to himself,—Ah! with what exquisite pleasure could I feast upon his flesh!—Be it so; but first let me remove all suspicion. So having thus resolved, he advanced towards him, and said,—Peace be with thee, friend! Who art thou? said the deer. I am Kshudrabudhee,† the jackal, said he; and being without relations, I dwell here in this forest, as it were, like one dead; but now that I have fallen in with a true friend, I am no longer destitute of connections, and am again entered into the land of the living; and henceforward it shall be my duty to attend thy steps.

Accordingly, as soon as the sun had retired to the western mountain, the jackal followed the deer to his place of residence, beneath the branches of the champaka tree, where with him lived also his friend the crow, whose name was Su-budhee.‡ Upon seeing him, the crow said, Who is this second? and the deer replied, It is a jackal, who is come here desirous of our friendship. Friend, said the crow, it is not

* A tree which bears a beautiful yellow flower of a very powerful and agreeable scent, known to Europeans by the name of Champak.

† Low-minded, mean-spirited, bad-hearted.

‡ Well-judging, good-hearted.

proper to place confidence in one who cometh without any apparent cause. It is not well done, for it is said:

To one whose family and profession are unknown, one should not give residence: the jackal Jarad-gava was killed through the fault of a cat.

How was this? said they; and the crow related as follows:

FABLE IV.

ON the banks of the river Bhageerathee, and upon the mountain Greedhra-koota, there is a large parkattee tree, in the hollow of whose trunk there dwelt a jackal, by name Jarad-gava, who, by some accident, was grown blind, and for whose support the different birds, who roosted upon the branches of the same tree, were wont to contribute a trifle from their own stores, by which he existed. It so fell out, that one day a certain cat, by name Deerga-karna,* came there to prey upon the young birds, whom perceiving, the little nestlings were greatly terrified, and began to be very clamorous; and their cries being heard by Jarad-gava, he asked who was coming. The cat Deerga-karna, too, seeing the jackal, began to be alarmed, and so cried to himself,—Oh! I shall certainly be killed, for now that I am in his sight, it will not be in my power to escape! However, let what will be the consequence, I will approach him. So having thus resolved, he went up to the jackal, and said,—Master, I salute thee! Who art thou? demanded the jackal. Said he, I am a cat. Ah! wicked animal, cried the jackal, get thee at a distance; for, if thou dost not, I will put thee to death. Hear me for a moment, replied puss, and then determine whether I merit either to be punished or to be killed.

'What, is any one, simply by birth, to be punished or applauded? When his deeds have been scrutinized, he may, indeed, be either praiseworthy or punishable.

'Men are the same as other animals, in eating, sleeping, fearing, and propagation. Reason, alone, is man's superior distinction. Deprived of reason, he is upon an equality with the brutes.'

The jackal after this desired the cat to give some account of himself, and he complied in the following words:—I am, said he, in the constant habit of performing ablutions on the side of this river; I never eat flesh, and I lead that mode of life which is called Brahma-charya.* So, as thou art distinguished amongst those of thy own species noted for skill in

* Forsaking all worldly concerns to lead a godly life.

religious matters, as a repository of confidence; and as the birds here are always speaking before me in praise of thy good qualities, I am come to hear from thy mouth, who art so old in wisdom, the duties of religion. Thou, master, art acquainted with the customs of life; but these young birds, who are in ignorance, would fain drive me, who am a stranger, away. The duties of a housekeeper* are thus enjoined:

'Hospitality is commanded to be exercised, even towards an enemy, when he cometh to thine house. The tree doth not withdraw its shade, even from the wood-cutter.'

And if there be no bread, the stranger should be entertained with kind words, and whatever can be spared, as in these lines:

'Some straw, a room, water, and in the fourth place, gentle words. These things are never to be refused in good men's houses.'

And in another verse it is said:

* The Hindoo divines ordain four modes of life, which are thus denominated:—*Brahma-charya*, *Graha-stha*, *Vana-prastha*, *Sannyasa*. The followers of the first mode live in society, but are not allowed any of its pleasures. Those of the second are the housekeepers, who are enjoined hospitality and every social duty. The third mode is retirement from society into the wilderness, as the term imports. And the fourth a total forsaking of all worldly things. Those who prefer the latter mode are, for the most part, wanderers. In the Dharama-Sastra of Manoo the particular duties of each are very fully treated of.

'The stranger, who turneth away from a house with disappointed hopes, leaveth there his own offences, and departeth, taking with him all the good actions of the owner.' *

Again:

'Fire † is the superior of the Brahmans, the Brahman is the superior of the tribes,‡ and the husband is the only superior of women; but the stranger is the superior of all.

'Good men extend their pity, even unto the most despicable animals. The moon doth not withhold the light, even from the cottage of a Chandala.' §

To all this the jackal replied,—Cats have a taste for animal food, and above is the residence of the young birds: it is on this account I speak to thee. The cat having touched her two ears, and then the

* This doctrine is strongly inculcated in every Hindoo system of morality, and, seemingly, with a very powerful effect; for a beggar is never seen to turn away from a door in India with disappointed hopes.

† This element, in ancient times, seems to have been universally deified. The Hindoos are enjoined by those laws they esteem of divine origin, at a certain period to light up a fire, which must be produced by the friction of two pieces of wood of a particular species, and to keep it up as long as they live. With this fire all their sacrifices are burnt, their nuptial altar flames, and, finally, the funeral pile is kindled.

‡ These tribes were, originally, only four: the *Brahman* (divines), *Kshetrees* (nobles and military), *Visyas* (cultivators of the land, herdsmen, merchants, and mechanics), and *Soodras* (menial servants).

§ An outcast. One of the very lowest order in society, employed in all the dirty offices for the four superior tribes.

ground,* exclaimed,—I who have read books upon the duties of religion, and am freed from inordinate desires, have forsaken such an evil practice; and, indeed, even amongst those who dispute with one another about the authority of the Sastras, there are many by whom this sentence, "Not to kill is a supreme duty," is altogether approved; as in this verse:

'Those who have forsaken the killing of all; those who are helpmates to all; those who are a sanctuary to all; those men are in the way to heaven.'

Again:

'There is one friend, even Religion,† who attendeth even in death; whilst all things else go to decay with the body.

'Behold the difference between the one who eateth flesh, and he to whom it belonged! The first hath a momentary enjoyment, whilst the latter is deprived of existence!'

So it is said,

'A fellow-creature should be spared, even by this analogy: the pain which a man suffereth when he is at the point of death.'

Hear this also:

'Who would commit so great a crime against a

* A very expressive way of declaring abhorrence.

† The original word (*dharma*) includes every moral and religious duty.

poor animal, who is fed only by the herbs which grow wild in the woods, and whose belly is burnt up with hunger?'

The cat by these means having satisfied him, he remained in the hollow of the tree with the jackal, and passed the time in amusing conversation; and the jackal told the young birds that they had no occasion to go out of the way.—After this, when many days had passed, it was discovered that the cat had, by degrees, drawn the little birds down into the hollow of the tree, and there devoured them; but when he found inquiry was about to be made by those whose young ones had been eaten, he slipped out of the hole and made his escape. In the meantime, the bones of the young ones having been discovered in the hollow of the tree by the birds, who had been searching here and there, they concluded that their little ones had been devoured by the jackal, and so, being joined by other birds, they put him to death. Wherefore I say,—"To one whose family and profession are unknown," &c.

The jackal having heard all this, replied in anger,—Hear me, thou fool! The first time thou wast seen by the deer, thy family and profession were unknown. How is it, then, that your mutual kindness and attention grow higher and higher?

'*Is this one of us, or is he a stranger?* Such is the

enumeration of the ungenerous ; but to those by whom liberality is practised, the whole world is but as one family.'

Wherefore, I say, be thou my acquaintance in the same manner the deer is. What is the use of all these replies? observed the deer. Let us dwell together, and spend our time happily in agreeable conversation.

'There is no one the friend of another ; there is no one the enemy of another : friends, as well as enemies, are created through our transactions.'

So, at length, the crow said,—Let it be so.

Early in the morning they used to go abroad to those parts they liked best. One day the jackal said to the deer, in great secrecy,—In a particular part of this wood, my friend, there is a field full of corn, to which I will conduct thee; and which being performed accordingly, the deer used to go there every day to feed upon the corn; but, in time, this being discovered by the master of the field, he laid snares for him. After this, the deer coming there again, and being confined in the snares, thus reasoned to himself: Who but a friend can deliver me from these snares of the huntsman, so like the snares of death? In the meantime, the jackal, having arrived at the spot, stopped short, and began to consider what he should do. So far, said he, my scheme has succeeded, and by means of these deceitful snares, my wishes will be accomplished in great abundance; for when he is cut up, I shall get his bones all covered with flesh and blood. The deer was exceedingly glad to see him, and called out to him,—Friend jackal, pray gnaw my bonds asunder, and speedily deliver me!

'A friend may be known in adversity, a hero in battle, an honest man in a loan, a wife when riches are spent, and a relation in trouble.'

The jackal eyed the deer in his confinement again and again, and considered whether the knots were secure. These snares, my friend, observed he, are made of leather thongs, and it being Sunday, how can I touch them with my teeth?* But, if it will suit thee, my friend, early in the morning I will do whatever may be thy wish. So having made this proposal, he went on one side, and laying himself down, remained silent.

In the meantime the crow, Subuddhi, finding the deer did not come home, had gone about in search of him. At length he found him in this condition, upon which he exclaimed,—What, my friend, is this the promise! Is this the fruit of the word of a friend!

* Good Hindoos esteem all animal substances unclean; but, the question is, why the jackal was scrupulous about touching them of a *Sunday*: unless it was out of respect to the *God of day*, after whom it is called.

'He who doth not hearken to the voice of a friend and well-wisher in adversity, is the delight of his enemies.'

But where is that jackal? added the crow. Alas! said the deer, he is here anxiously waiting for my flesh! My friend, observed the crow, I foretold this from the beginning.

'I am not to blame: he was not a subject for confidence. From the cruel, even the virtuous have cause for apprehension.'

Saying this, he heaved a deep sigh, and cried, O deceitful wretch! what hath been brought to pass by thee, thou agent of wickedness!

'How hard is disappointment in this world, to such as have been deluded by fair words; to those who by pretended services have been seduced into the power of their enemies; to the hopeful; to those who have faith, and to expectants!

'A man should forsake such a friend as speaketh kindly to his face, and behind his back defeateth his designs. He is like a pot of poison with a surface of milk.

'O goddess Vasudha!* How supportest thou that treacherous man, who exerciseth his wickedness upon his innocent and confidential companion!'

* The earth.

Is not this, continued the crow, the character of bad men?

'A man should not form any acquaintance, nor enter into any amusements, with one of an evil character. A piece of charcoal, if it be hot, burneth; and if cold, it blackeneth the hand.

'Although one of an evil character speak kindly, that is no motive for his being trusted. The serpent is ornamented with a gem,* but is he not to be dreaded?

'Before one's face, he falleth at one's feet; behind, he biteth the flesh of one's back. In one's ear, doth he not softly hum his tune with wondrous art! And when he findeth a hole, fearless, he boldly entereth. Thus doth the gnat † perform the actions of a deceitful man.'

About this time the owner of the field was seen coming, with a staff in his hand, and his eyes red with anger. So the crow, having considered what was to be done, said,—Friend deer, feign thyself dead, and stay quiet till I make a noise, and then get up and run away as fast as thou canst. The deer

* It is a vulgar notion in India that in the heads of some species of serpents precious stones are found.

† The word in the original signifies a *mosquito*, which, as far as the translator has carried his observations since his return to his native country, is no ways different from the common English gnat, except that it makes a louder noise, and is more venomous.

was now perceived by the master of the field, whose eyes sparkled with joy; but upon his approaching nearer, and thinking him dead, he exclaimed,—Ha! thou art dead of thyself from confinement, art thou? and having said so, he began to employ himself in collecting and bundling up his snares; and upon his moving to a little distance, the deer hearing the voice of the crow, started up in great disorder, and ran away. The master of the field, upon seeing this, flung his staff at him, which, by chance, struck the jackal, and so he was killed, and not the deer. It is said, that

'A man reapeth the fruit of any extraordinary good or bad action in the space of three years, three months, three fortnights,* or three days.

'Wherefore I repeat, "Harmony between the food and the feeder," &c.'

To all this the crow replied:

'In eating thee, I should not enjoy a plenteous meal. But, like Chitra-greeva, I live but in thy life.

'Even amongst brutes, confidence is perceived in those, in whose every action there is innocence. The innate disposition of the good doth not vary from the principles of integrity.

* The Hindoos have divided their lunar month into what they denominate the *sookla-paksha*, and the *kreeshna-paksha*, that is, the *light side* and the *dark side* (of the moon); the former commences with the new moon, and the latter with the full.

'The mind of a good man doth not alter, even when he is in distress: the waters of the ocean are not to be heated by a torch of straw.'

But, friend crow, observed the mouse Hiranyaka, thou art an unsteady and inconstant animal, and one's affections should, on no account, be placed on such a character; as is declared in these lines:

'A cat, a buffalo, a ram, a crow, and a man of weak judgment are excluded from confidence: it is not expedient to put any trust in them.'

Besides, thou art on the side of our enemies, and on this head they say,

'A man should not enter into alliance with his enemy, even with the tightest bonds of union. Water made ever so hot, will still quench fire.'

And again:

'That is not possible which is impossible. That which is possible is ever possible. A cart moveth not upon the waters, nor a boat upon dry ground.'

I have heard every book upon these subjects, said the crow Laghu-patanaka, nevertheless my mind is impressed with this idea, that I must absolutely form a friendly acquaintance with thee; but if I should fail, after our separation I shall destroy myself. It is said, that those of evil character are like an earthen pot—easy to be broken, but hard to be re-united;

and that those of a good character resemble a vessel of gold, which, though difficult to be broken, may easily be joined again. It is said,

'Metals unite from fluxility; birds and beasts from motives of convenience; fools from fear and stupidity; and just men at sight.

'Although friendship between good men be interrupted, still their principles remain unaltered. The stalk of the lotus may be broken, and the fibres remain connected.

'The qualities of a friend should be, sincerity, liberality, bravery, constancy in joy and sorrow, rectitude, attachment, veracity.'

Whom, then, but thyself shall I find endued with all these?

Upon hearing this, Hiranyaka slipped out of his hole, and said,—Well, by the immortal water of thy words, I have even ventured out; for it is said,

'Nor bathing with cool water, nor a necklace of pearls,* nor anointing with sanders,† yieldeth such comfort to the body oppressed with heat, as the language of a good man, cheerfully uttered, doth to

* Strings of beads formed of various materials are universally worn about the neck in India, by men, women, and children.

† The Hindoos never wash in the Ganges, but they mark themselves on the forehead, across the arms, and upon the breast, with a kind of pigment made of the white species of sanders, or sandal wood, mixed with water, which they suffer to dry on.

the mind. To be surrounded with a good connection is, amongst men of fair character, equal to the charm of attraction.' *

And in another place:

'Betraying a secret, insolicitude, severity, insensibility, anger, want of veracity, gaming: all these are faults in a friend.'

But of all these faults in due order, not one is to be found in thee. It is said,

'Eloquence, and veracity of speech, are to be discovered by conversation; the being inimical with inconstancy or unsteadiness, may be perceived at sight.

'The friendship of those who are of a pure and gentle disposition, acteth one way; and that of those whose hearts are affected with hollowness and deceit, another.'

Then, as long as we both shall live, so long let this our friendship be nourished, like that which existed between Rama and Sugreeva.†

So Hiranyaka having promised his friendship, and entertained the crow with such provisions as he

* What the nature of the charm alluded to may be, the translator is at a loss to explain.

† A baboon celebrated in the "Ramayan," or history of Ram, as his faithful friend and ally, in his wars against Ravana, the tyrant of Ceylon.

had, retired into his hole; and the crow also retired to his usual place of abode.

From that time there existed a mutual friendship between them. Day after day passed away in making presents to one another of provisions, and the like; in reciprocal inquiries after each other's health, and in amusing conversation. One day the crow said to the mouse,—Friend Hiranyaka, provisions are very difficult to be procured in this place, wherefore I am about to abandon it, to repair to some other. Hiranyaka replied,

'Teeth, hair, nails, and the human species, prosper not when separated from their place. A wise man being informed of this, should not totally forsake his native home.'

Friend, observed the crow, this is the sentiment of weak men; for it is said,

'Wise men, lions, and elephants, quit one place and go to another; whilst crows, weak men, and the deer species, meet death in the same place.'

Then, whither shall we go? demanded Hiranyaka. They say,

'A wise man moveth with one foot, and standeth fast with the other. A man should not quit one place until he hath fixed upon another.'

Said the crow: There is a place well thought of.

Where is it? replied the mouse; and the crow replied,—In Dandakaranya there is a river celebrated by the name Karpooragow, where there resides my friend, by many years accumulated kindness, a tortoise of innate virtue, whose name is Manthara. It is said,

'In giving advice to another, the experience of every one may be beneficial; but in religion, the proper example of some one of a very exalted mind.'

He will treat us, added the crow, with a variety of choice fish. Hiranyaka then said,—If I stay here, what shall I do? It is said,

'A man should abandon that country, wherein there is neither respect, nor employment, nor connections, nor the advancement of science.'

Again:

'A man should not reside in a place, wherein these five things are not to be found: wealthy inhabitants, Brahmans learned in the Vedas, a rajah,* a river, and, in the fifth place, a physician.'

* In the ancient Hindoo government, before the Mussulman conquest, which seems to have been feudal, this title was granted by the superior lord, who was styled Maha-Rajah (great Rajah), or Adheeswara (superior lord), to the chiefs of the Kshetree or military tribe only, as a reward for merit, or as an appendage of office, with the ceremony of sprinkling consecrated water upon the head; but at present the *firman* of the king of Delhi is, but too often, issued to ennoble collectors of

So conduct me there also, added the mouse.

The crow accordingly set off with his friend, and as they amused the time by conversing upon a variety of pleasing subjects, they arrived with ease upon the banks of the river. They were perceived at a considerable distance by the tortoise Manthara. He rose to receive them, and having first performed the duties of hospitality to Laghu-patanaka, he next extended them to Hiranyaka; according to these lines:

'Whether a child, or an old man, or a youth, be come to thy house, he is to be treated with respect; for of all men, thy guest is the superior.

'Fire is the superior of the Brahmans, the Brahman is the superior of the tribes, and the husband is the only superior of women; but the stranger is the superior of all.

'Whether he who is come to thy house be of the highest or even of the lowest rank in society, he is worthy to be treated with due respect; for of all men thy guest is the superior.'

Friend, said the crow to the tortoise, pray pay attention to this stranger; for he is the very axis of those who are famed for virtuous deeds. His name is Hiranyaka, the prince of mice, to celebrate whose

revenue, and wretches of the lowest class, destitute of every merit but that of immense wealth. The term is derived from a root signifying *to appear with splendour*.

great qualities, the chief of serpents * may sometimes have occasion to employ a second thousand tongues. Having said this, he related the story of the pigeon Chitra-greeva. The tortoise Manthara, having made respectful inquiries after his health, said to the mouse,—Be pleased to inform me of thy motives for quitting thy own uninhabited wilds; and Hiranyaka replied, I will recount them.

FABLE V.

BE it known, said he, that there is a city called Champakavatee, where many mendicants are wont to resort. Amongst the rest there was one whose name was Choorakarna.† This mendicant, having placed the dish containing what was left of the alms he collected upon a forked stick fixed in the wall, used to go to sleep, whilst I, every day, contrived to jump from a distance and devour the hoard. At length, one day his friend, another mendicant, whose name was Veenakarna, came in, and whilst he was engaged with him talking over various subjects, Choorakarna, in order to frighten me away, struck the ground with a piece of bamboo. This being observed by Veenakarna, he said,—What, at present, thou art inattentive to my

* The serpent Sesh or Ananta. Employing the emblem of eternity with a thousand tongues in the character of Fame, is not ill imagined.

† Ring-ear.

story, and employed about something else? It is said,

'A pleasant countenance, and a mien without pride; great attention to what is said, and sweetness of speech; a great degree of kindness, and the appearance of awe; are always tokens of a man's attachment.'

So,

'Giving unwillingly, rendering void what he did before, disrespectful behaviour, unkind actions, praising others, and, by the assistance of tales, calumniating behind one's back, are the signs of one who is not attached.'

To all this Choorakarna replied,—I am not inattentive to thy story. Behold what it is! This mouse is my plunderer. He is for ever devouring the meat I get by begging, out of that dish. Upon this, Veenakarna having examined the forked stick in the wall, said,—What, is it this little weak-looking mouse who contrives to jump so very far? There must be some reason to account for this; as in the subject of these lines:

Without an apparent cause, a young woman by force draweth an old man to her, and kisseth him. When a husband is embraced without affection, there must be some reason for it.

Choorakarna having demanded what this meant, Veenakarna related the following story:

FABLE VI.

IN the country which is called Gowr,* there is a city, by name Kowsamvee, where dwelt Chandana-dama, a merchant of immense wealth. When in the last stage of life, his understanding being blinded by desire, by the glare of his riches he obtained for his wife Leelavatee,† the daughter of another merchant. She was youthful, and, as it were, the victorious banner of Makaraketu,‡ the god of love; so her aged partner was ill calculated to be agreeable to her; for,

'As the hearts of those who are pinched with cold, delight not in the rays of the moon; nor of those who are oppressed with heat, in the beams of the sun; so the heart of a woman delighteth not in a husband stricken in years.'

Again:

'What name shall we give to the passions of men, when their hairs are turned grey; since women, with their hearts fixed on others, regard them as a nauseous drug?'

* The ancient city of Gowr, which is now in ruins, was the capital of a province of the same name, now included in that of Bengal.

† Sportive, wanton.

‡ One of the titles of the Hindoo Cupid, who is commonly called Kama-deva, the god of love.

But her old husband was exceedingly fond of her; according to these sayings:

'The lust of wealth, and the hope of life, are ever of importance to man; but a youthful wife to an old man is dearer than life itself.'

Nevertheless, Leelavatee, through the intoxication of youth, attached herself to a certain merchant's son.

'Too much liberty whilst resident in her father's house, attending festive processions, appearing in company in the presence of men contrary to propriety, the same in byways, and associating with women of bad character, are the immediate destruction of innate morals. Sporting with their husbands' infirmities, too, is to women the cause of ruin.'

Again:

'Drinking, keeping bad company, staying away from her husband, gadding about, slothfulness, and living at another's house, are six things injurious to a woman.

'Women, at all times, have been inconstant; even amongst the celestials, we are told. Happy is the portion of those men whose wives are guarded from error!

'Women's virtue is founded upon a modest countenance, precise behaviour, rectitude, and the want of suitors.'

They say,

'Woman is like a pot of oil, and man a burning coal. A wise man will not put the oil and the fire together.

'In infancy the father should guard her, in youth her husband should guard her, and in old age her children should guard her; for, at no time, is a woman proper to be trusted with liberty.'

One day, as she was carelessly sitting with the merchant's son, in agreeable conversation, upon a sofa white as camphire, and fringed with strings of gems, having unexpectedly discovered her husband coming towards them, she rose up in a great hurry, seized him by the hair, and eagerly embracing, began to kiss him; whilst the gallant found means to escape. But one who saw this understood her motive, and Leelavatee was corrected by a hidden rod.*

'Every book of knowledge which is known to Usana, or to Vrihaspati, is by nature planted in the understanding of women.'

Upon the whole, I say, "Without a cause a young woman," &c. And hence there must be some hidden cause for the extraordinary strength of this mouse. He considered for a moment, and at length determined that the reason must be in a hoard of wealth: for,

* That is, she was obliged to silence the woman with hush money.

'In this world the wealthy are, every one, everywhere, and at all times, powerful. Riches are the foundation of preferment, and an introduction to the prince.'

Having said this, a spade was brought, and my hole being dug open by that mendicant, the hoard which I had been accumulating for many years was carried away! After this, day by day, my strength decreased, and having little power to exert myself, I was unable to procure even sufficient to support life; and in this condition, as I was fearfully and feebly skulking about, I was observed by Choorakarna, upon which he repeated the following lines:

'With wealth all are powerful; from wealth a man is esteemed learned. Behold this wicked mouse! see how he is reduced to the natural level of his species!

'Deprived of riches, all the actions of a man of little judgment disappear, like trifling streams in the summer's heat.'

And again:

'He who hath riches hath friends; he who hath riches hath relations; he who hath riches is a man of consequence in the world; he who hath riches is esteemed a learned man.

'The house of the childless is empty; and so is the heart of him who hath no wife. The mind of a fool is empty; and everything is empty, where there is poverty.'

They say also,

'"Those faculties are not injured." This is a mere saying. "That judgment is unimpaired." That also is but an expression; for the moment a man is deprived of the comfort of riches, he is quite another. Is not this curious?'

Having heard all this, I looked about me, and resolved that it would not, by any means, be proper for me to stay there: neither, by-the-by, is it proper that I should communicate my affairs to others; for,

'A wise man should not make known the loss of fortune, any malpractices in his house; his being cheated, nor his having been disgraced.'

They say, likewise,

'When the frowns of fortune are excessive, and human endeavours are exerted in vain; where, but in the wilderness, can comfort be found for a poor man of sensibility?

'A man of nice feelings willingly encountereth death, rather than submit to poverty. A fire meeteth extinction, before it will yield to be cold.'

Again:

'The fate of a man of feeling is, like that of a tuft

of flowers, twofold: he may either mount upon the head of all, or go to decay in the wilderness.'

To live despised is reprobated exceedingly. Hence,

'It is better that the (funeral) fire should be blown up by the breath of life* of a man deprived of riches, than that he should be solicited by the poor, when destitute of the means of relief.'

Again:

'From poverty a man cometh to shame; and being overwhelmed with disgrace, he is totally deprived of power. Without power he is oppressed, and from oppression cometh grief. Loaded with grief, he becometh melancholy; and impaired by melancholy, he is forsaken by reason; and with the loss of reason, he goeth to destruction. Alas! the want of riches is the foundation of every misfortune.'

Again:

'It is better to guard silence, than that the words which are uttered should be untrue. It is better to be nothing, than to seduce the wife of another. It is better to abandon life, than to delight in cruel conversation. It is better to live by begging one's bread, than to gratify the mouth at the expense of others.'

* Death itself is preferable to the want of the means of affording relief to those in distress.

Want maketh even servitude honourable; light, total darkness; beauty, deformity; and even the words of Hari, with a hundred good qualities, crimes. What then, shall I nourish myself with another's cake? This would be to open a second door to death. For,

'When a man is in indigence, picking herbs is his philosophy;* the enjoyment of his wife his only commerce, and vassalage his food.'

Again:

'Death is life to him who is subject to sickness, who hath been long an exile, who liveth upon another's bread, or sleepeth under another's roof; for death easeth him of all his pain.'

Having considered all this, I have again, through covetousness, made up my mind to accept of some of thy provisions. But it is said,

'With covetousness reason departeth: covetousness engendereth avarice; and the man who is tormented with avarice experienceth pain, both here and hereafter.'

Hence, after I had been struck with the broken piece of bamboo by Veenakarna, I began to consider, that

* There is no word in the Sanskrit which answers exactly to this term The original is *panditya*, an abstract formed from *pandit*.

the covetous were unhappy, and assuredly their own enemy. It is said,

'He whose mind is at ease is possessed of all riches. Is it not the same to one whose foot is enclosed in a shoe, as if the whole surface of the earth were covered with leather?'

Again:

'Where have they, who are running here and there in search of riches, such happiness as those placid spirits enjoy, who are gratified at the immortal fountain of happiness?

'All hath been read, all hath been heard, and all hath been followed by him, who having put hope behind him, dependeth not upon expectation.

'Fortunate is the life of that man, by whom the door of the noble hath not been attended; by whom the pain of separation hath not been experienced; and by whom the voice of an eunuch* hath not been heard.'

Again:

'To one, O Narada,† borne away by the thirst of gain, a hundred Yojana appear not far; even after he hath the treasure in his hand.'

* How greatly do the tastes of nations differ!

† One of the seven wise men, to whom is attributed the invention of the musical instrument called *veena*.

It is good, then, to be entirely separated far from the usual occasions of life.

'What is religion? Compassion for all things which have life. What is happiness? To animals in this world, health. What is kindness? A principle in the good. What is philosophy? An entire separation from the world.'

It is said,

'A man may forsake one person to save a family; he may desert a whole family for the sake of a village; and sacrifice a village for the safety of the community; but for himself he may abandon the whole world.'

But,

'To those who seek employment, it is esteemed a favour to be an appendage only of a great man's station. The serpent Vasukee * is contented to feed on air, whilst hanging to the neck of Hara.†

'It is, either water without labour, or sweet bread attended by fear and danger. I have examined this; and I plainly see, that is happiness wherein there is ease.'

So, having considered all this, I am come to an uninhabited wilderness; for,

* The serpent employed in churning the ocean for the water of life.

† One of the titles of Seeva, the destroying power of the deity, who is represented with a large snake about his neck by way of necklace; a proper ornament for the God of Terrors.

'It is better to dwell in a forest haunted by tigers and lions, the trees our habitation, flowers, fruits and water for food, the grass for a bed, and the bark of the trees for garments, than to live amongst relations, after the loss of wealth.'

Wherefore, as long as the stock of virtue acquired by birth shall last,* I will, with this true friend, be attached to thee by kind services; and by this single virtuous act, I may obtain that place in heaven which is consecrated to friendship.† They say,

'Of the poisonous tree, the world, two species of fruit are produced, sweet as the water of life: poetry, whose taste is like the immortal juice, and the society of good men.'

Again:

'Society, faith in Kesava,‡ and immerging in the waters of the Ganges, may be esteemed three very essential things in this transitory world.

'Riches are as the dust of the feet, youth like the rapidity of a river flowing down a hill, manhood like

* This sentence is agreeable to the notion, that the joys of heaven are to last for a period measured by our good actions in this life.

† The Hindoo divines have divided heaven into different regions which they call *lok.* Thus there is the *pitri-lok*, or region of fathers, and the *matri-lok*, or region of mothers; but there is no region allotted for old maids and bachelors: these are obliged to renew their youth in this life, and try their luck once more.

‡ One of the names of Vishnu in his incarnation of Kreeshna.

a drop of water, transient and unsteady;* and human life like froth. He who doth not perform the duties of religion, with a steady mind, to open the bars of Heaven's gate, will, hereafter, when smitten with sorrow, and bent down with old age, burn with the fire of contrition.'

To all this the tortoise Manthara replied,—Sir, your fault was this: you laid up too large a stock. It is said,

'Giving away is the instrument for accumulated treasures: it is like a bucket for the distribution of the waters deposited in the bowels of a well.

'He who, in opposition to his own happiness, delighteth in the accumulation of riches, carrieth burthens for others, and is the vehicle of trouble.'

Another:

'If we are rich with the riches of which we neither give nor enjoy, we are rich with the riches which are buried in the caverns of the earth.

'Without enjoyment, the wealth of the miser is the same to him as if it were another's. But when it is

* A drop of water upon a leaf of the lotus, must be understood; agreeable to the following hemistich engraved on a copper-plate bearing date fifty-six years before the Christian era, and which, about the year 1781, was sent from India as a present to Lord Mansfield:

"Riches and the life of man are transient as drops of water upon a leaf of the lotus."—Translated by C. W. 1781.

said of a man, "he hath so much," it is with difficulty he can be induced to part with it.'

They say,

'The wealth of the miser goeth neither to the celestials,* nor to the Brahmans, nor to his kindred, nor to himself; but to the fire, the thief, and the magistrate.'

And,

'He who eateth by measure, whilst his treasure is buried low in the ground, is preparing for a journey to a mansion below.' †

So,

'Giving with kind words, knowledge without pride, heroism accompanied by clemency, and wealth with liberality, are four excellences hard to be found.'

It is said,

A hoard should always be made; but not too great a hoard. A jackal, through the fault of hoarding too much, was killed by a bow.

How was this? demanded Hiranyaka; and Manthara related the following story:

* In sacrifices and other expensive ceremonies.

† The Hindoos place their hell, which seems to be but for a temporary punishment, in the bowels of the earth.

FABLE VII.

A CERTAIN huntsman, by name Bhirava, an inhabitant of Kalyana-kattaka,* being fond of flesh, once upon a time went to hunt in the forests of the Vindhya mountains,† and having killed a deer, as he was carrying him away, he chanced to see a wild boar of a formidable appearance. So laying the deer upon the ground, he wounded the boar with an arrow; but, upon his approaching him, the horrid animal set up a roar dreadful as the thunder of the clouds, and wounding him in the groin, he fell like a tree cut off by the axe. At the same time, a serpent, of that species which is called Ajagara, pressed by hunger and wandering about, rose up and bit the boar, who instantly fell helpless upon him, and remained upon the spot. For,

'The body having encountered some efficient cause, water, fire, poison, the sword, hunger, sickness, or a fall from an eminence, is forsaken by the vital spirits.'

In the meantime, a jackal, by name Deergha-rava,‡ prowling about in search of prey, discovered the deer, the huntsman, and the boar; and having observed

* Probably an ancient name for the province we call Cattack.
† That chain which is seen about Chunar-ghur.
‡ Long-cry.

them, he said to himself,—Here is a fine feast prepared for me.

'As, to corporeal beings, unthought-of troubles arrive; so, in like manner, do blessings make their appearance. In this, I think providence hath extended them farther than usual.'

Be it so, as long as with their flesh I shall have food to eat. The man will last me for a whole month, and the deer and the boar for two more; then the serpent will serve me a day; and let me taste the bow-string too. But, in the first place, let me try that which is the least savoury. Suppose, then, I eat this catgut line which is fastened to the bow: saying so, he drew near to eat it; but the instant he had bit the gut in two, his belly was ripped open by the spring of the bow; and he was reduced to the state of the five elements.* I say, therefore, "A hoard," &c.

'That I esteem wealth which is given to the worthy, and what is, day by day, enjoyed; the rest is a reserve for one knoweth not whom.'

Then, at present, what is the purport of this excessive use of the force of words to exemplify?

'Men of philosophic minds do not long for what is not attainable, and are not willing to lament what is

* Earth, air, fire, water, and ether.

lost; neither are they wont to be embarrassed in times of calamity.

'Those who have even studied good books, may still be fools. That man is learned who reduceth his learning to practice. That medicine is well imagined which doth, more than nominally, restore the health of the afflicted.

'The precepts of philosophy effect not the least benefit to one confirmed in fear. To a blind man, of what use is a lamp, although it be burning in his hand?'

After all, added the tortoise, it is best to be satisfied in this region of good and evil destiny.

I cannot agree to that, replied Hiranyaka; for,

'To a hero of a sound mind, what is his own, and what a foreign country? Wherever he halteth, that place is acquired by the splendour of his arms. He quencheth his thirst with the blood of the royal elephant, even in the forest which the lion teareth up with his teeth, and his claws the weapons of his feet.'

Again:

'As frogs to the pool, as birds to a lake full of water; so doth every species of wealth necessarily flow to the hands of him who exerteth himself.'

They say,

'When pleasure is arrived, it is worthy of attention; when trouble presenteth itself, the same. Pains and pleasures have their revolutions like a wheel!'

Again:

'Lakshmee* herself attendeth a man in search of a residence, who is endued with resolution, of noble principles, acquainted with the rules of action, untainted with lawless pleasures, brave, a judge of merit, and of steady friendship.'

Again:

'A wise man, even destitute of riches, enjoyeth elevated and very honourable stations; whilst the wretch, endowed with wealth, acquireth the post of disgrace.

'One, although not possessed of a mine of gold, may find the offspring of his own nature, that noble ardour, which hath for its object the accomplishment of the whole assemblage of virtues.'

Hear this, my friend, replied the tortoise:

'What, though thou wert rich and of high esteem, dost thou yield to sorrow, because of thy loss of fortune? The risings and sinkings of human affairs are like those of a ball which is thrown by the hand.'

Observe,

'The shadow of a cloud, the satisfaction of the

* The goddess of good fortune.

vulgar, new corn, women, youth, and riches, are to be enjoyed but for a short time.'

Again:

'Man should not be over-anxious for a subsistence, for it is provided by the Creator. The infant no sooner droppeth from the womb, than the breasts of the mother begin to stream.'

My friend:

'He, by whom the geese were formed white, parrots are stained green, and peacocks painted of various hues—even He will provide for their support.'

Attend also, my friend, to these secrets of the wise men:

'How are riches the means of happiness? In acquiring they create trouble, in their loss they occasion sorrow, and they are the cause of endless divisions amongst kindred!

'It were a blessing, for the sake of virtue, if he who hath a lust of gain were deprived of desire. Where there is a splashing of dirt, it is good not to meddle, and to keep far away.

'As meat is devoured by the birds in the air, by the beasts in the field, and by the fishes in the waters; so, in every situation, there is plenty.

'The rich man hath cause of fear, from the magistrate, from water, from fire, from the robber, not less from his own people, even as from death the living.

'In this life of many troubles, what pain is greater than this?—desire without ability, when that desire turneth not away!

'Man should consider this: That riches are not easily acquired; when acquired, they are with difficulty preserved; and that the loss of what hath been acquired is like death.'

So also:

'Were the thirst of gain entirely forsaken, who would be poor? Who would be rich? If way were given to it, slavery would stand upon the head.

'Whatever a man should long for, from that his inclination turneth away. He whose inclination turneth away from an object, may be said to have obtained it.'

But why so much upon this subject? Let us beguile the time together in amusing conversation.

'Men who are acquainted with their own nature, pass their days, until the period of death, in gladness, free from anger, in the enjoyment of the present moment, unmindful of the world, and free from apprehension.'

Again:

'The life of an animal, until the hour of his death,

passeth away in disciplines, in elevations and depressions, in unions and separations.'

O! thou art a worthy person, Manthara, observed the crow; a place of confidence, and a being for protection!

'The good are always ready to be the upholders of the good in their misfortunes. Elephants even are wont to bear the burthens of elephants who have sunk in the mire.'

So,

'The virtuous delight in the virtuous; but he who is destitute of the practice of virtue, delighteth not in the virtuous. The bee retireth from the forest to the lotus, whilst the frog is destitute of a shelter.'

Again:

'He is one in this world worthy to be praised of mankind, he is a great and a good man, from whom the needy, or those who come for protection, go not away with disappointed hopes, and discontented countenances.'

In this manner did they pass their time; and, contented with their particular food, they dwelt happily together.

After a while, one day a certain deer, by name Vichitranga, who had been alarmed by some one, joined by the rest; but as they expected that he was pursued by something which had been the cause of his apprehensions, Manthara went into the water, the mouse into a hole, and the crow flew to the top of a tree. Laghu-patanaka looked on all sides; and being satisfied respecting their fears, they all joined company again. Health! friend deer, said the tortoise, thou art welcome. Mayst thou find provisions to thy heart's desire in this situation! May this forest never be rendered the property of a master!

To this the deer Chitranga replied,—I was alarmed by a huntsman, and I am come to you for protection.

'It is declared by the wise men, that the crime of him who shall forsake one who, through want or danger, may come to him for protection, is the same as the murder of a Brahman.'

And I wish also to cultivate a friendship with you. Sir, said the mouse, your friendship with us is accomplished without much trouble; for,

'Friends are said to be of four distinctions: one's own offspring, a connection, one descended from the same genealogical series, and one whom we may have preserved from misfortunes.'

So let us dwell together, added the mouse, without distinction.

The deer, upon hearing this, was rendered happy

He ate of what was his usual food, and having drank some water, he laid himself down in the shade of a tree which grew in the stream.

'Well water, the shade of a Batta tree,* a swarthy woman, and a brick house, should be warm in the cold, and cool in the hot season.'

Friend deer, said the tortoise Manthara, by whom wert thou alarmed? What, are there huntsmen coming to this desolate forest? There is some very important news, said the deer, which I will communicate. In the country which is called Kalinga † there is a prince whose name is Rukmangada.‡ He is just returned from his conquests of the countries about him, and his anger being altogether appeased, he has taken up his residence upon the banks of the river Chandra-bhaga. To-morrow early he has resolved to come to fish in the river Karphoora. This I overheard from the mouth of one of the sportsmen. Having investigated this affair, so much to be dreaded, let the necessary means be pursued for our safety. The tortoise upon hearing these words fearfully exclaimed,—I will flee to the water for protection! The crow and the

* The Banian tree.

† Probably the ancient name of a district on the coast of Coromandel.

‡ Golden elephant.

deer said,—Be it so. The mouse Hiranyaka considered for a moment, and said,

'When Manthara shall be in the water, it will be good for him. It appeareth to me improper that he should be found crawling upon dry ground.'

They say,

'The strength of aquatic animals is the waters; of those who dwell in towns, a castle; of foot-soldiers, their own ground; of princes, an obedient army.'

But, friend Laghu-patanaka, I hope by this advice, he will not suffer the regret experienced by a certain merchant.*

How was this? said they;—and Hiranyaka recounted as follows:

FABLE VIII.

IN the country of Kanya-kubja there was a Rajah, whose name was Veera-sena,† by whom his royal son, by name Tunga-vala,‡ had been appointed Yuva-rajah§ over the city of Veera-pura. He was young and possessed of great riches. Once upon a time, as he was walking about his own city, he took

* The verse which usually introduces the fable, being in this place very defective, is omitted.

† Whose troops are brave.

‡ From *tunga*, fierce, and *vala*, strength.

§ Literally Young Rajah. The title formerly borne by the heir apparent.

notice of a certain merchant's wife, who was in the very prime of youth, and so beautiful, that she was, as it were, the standard of conquest of Makara-ketu. She also, whose name was Lavanyavatee,* having observed him, her breast was rent in pieces by the destructive arrows of the god of love, and she gladly became of one mind with him. It is said,

'Unto women no man is to be found disagreeable, no one agreeable. They may be compared to a heifer on the plain, that still longeth for fresh grass.

'Infidelity, violence, deceit, envy, extreme avariciousness, a total want of good qualities, with impurity, are the innate faults of womankind.' †

The young Rajah being returned to his palace, with a heart quite occupied with love, sent a female messenger to her, to whose words having attended, Lavanyavatee made such a reply as was calculated to deceive. Said she,—I am faithful to my husband, and I am not accustomed even to touch another man; for,

'She is not worthy to be called a wife, in whom the husband delighteth not. The husband is the

* Beautiful.

† The fair reader will please to observe that this severe judgment of the sex was probably written by one under a vow of perpetual celibacy.

asylum of women; and of his honour the fire beareth testimony.*

'The beauty of the Kokila† is his voice; the beauty of a wife is constancy to her husband; the beauty of the ill-favoured is science; the beauty of the penitent is patience.

'She is a wife who is clever in the house; she is a wife who is fruitful in children; she is a wife who is the soul of her husband; she is a wife who is obedient to her husband.'

And according to this doctrine, I make it a rule to do whatever the lord of my life directs, without examination. To this the messenger replied,—It is right; and Lavanyavatee observed, that it was even so.

The messenger having heard the whole of what Lavanyavatee had to say, reported it to Tungavala, who observed that he would invite her with that dear husband of hers, and, in his presence, pay her great attention and respect. To this the messenger replied,—This is impracticable. Let art be used; for it is said,

* This sentence alludes to the ordeal by fire, which is practised, even at this time, in India.

† A black bird, very common in India, which sings in the night, and whose notes are as various and melodious as the nightingale's, but much louder.

That which cannot be effected by force may be achieved by cunning. An elephant was killed by a jackal, by going over a swampy place.

How was this? demanded the Rajah's son. And the messenger related the following story:

FABLE IX.

IN the forest Brahmaranya there was an elephant, whose name was Karphooratilaka,* who having been observed by the jackals, they all determined, that if he could by any stratagem be killed, he would be four months provisions for them all. One of them, who was exceedingly viciously inclined, and by nature treacherous, declared, that he would engage, by the strength of his own judgment, to effect his death. Some time after, this deceitful wretch went up to the elephant, and having saluted him, said,—Godlike sir! Condescend to grant me an audience. Who art thou? demanded the elephant, and whence comest thou? My name, replied he, is Kshudrabuddhi,† a jackal, sent into thy presence by all the inhabitants of the forest, assembled for that purpose, to represent, that as it is not expedient to reside in so large a forest as this, without a chief, your High-

* Marked with white spots.

† Low-minded, mean-spirited, bad-hearted.

ness, endued with all the cardinal virtues, hath been selected to be anointed Rajah of the woods.

It is said,

'He who, by walking for ever in the ways of those who are preferred, is exceedingly pure, of a noble mind, virtuous and just, and experienced in the rules of policy, is worthy to be chosen master of the earth.'

Again:

'The lord of the land, like the clouds, is the reservoir of the people; for when the clouds fail, do they not find succour in their king?'

But,

'In this world, which is subject to the power of One above, a man of good principles is hard to be found living in a country for the most part governed by the use of the rod.

'From the dread of the rod, like a woman of good repute unto her husband, he will repair for protection even unto the weak or unfortunate; to the sick, or to the poor.'

Then, that we may not lose the lucky moment, continued the jackal, be pleased to follow quickly. Saying this, he cocked his tail and went away. The elephant, whose reason was perverted by the lust of power, took the same road as the jackal, and followed him so exactly that, at length, he stuck fast in a great mire. O my friend! cried the elephant, what is to be done in this disaster? I am sinking in a deep mire! The jackal laughed, and said,—Please your divine Highness, take hold of my tail with your trunk, and get out! This is the fruit of those words which thou didst place confidence in.

They say,

'As often as thou shalt be deprived of the society of the good, so often shalt thou fall into the company of knaves.'

After a few days, the elephant dying for want of food, his flesh was devoured by the jackals. I say, therefore, "That which cannot be effected by force," &c.

The young Rajah, by the advice of his messenger, sent for the husband of Lavanyavatee, and having treated him with great marks of attention, took him into his service, and employed him in the most confidential affairs. One day, when the young Rajah had bathed and anointed himself, and was clothed in robes of gold, he said to the husband,—Charudanta, I am going to give a feast to the goddess Gowree,*

* Gowree is one of the names of the consort of Seeva; but as the same word means *a young woman* (literally, *a fair one*), it will agree better with the context, if the reader will be so good as to substitute, *to the young woman*, instead of *to the goddess Gowree*.

which will last for a month, and this evening it shall commence. Go then, and, just before night, bring to me a young maiden of singular beauty; and when she hath been presented, she shall have due respect paid to her, according to what is ordained. Charudanta did as he was commanded, and brought to his master such a young woman as he had described; and having delivered her, he privately resolved to find out how she was treated. The young Rajah, Tungavala, caused the young woman to sit down upon a rich sofa; and having entertained her with costly presents of cloth and garments, and given her a keepsake, he, that instant, sent her to her own house. Charudanta having been a spectator of all which had passed, said to himself,—This is a man of strict principles, who regardeth the woman of another as his own mother. So after that, through the confidence created by this stratagem, his mind being biassed by the lust of gain, he fetched his own wife and presented her; and the young Rajah upon beholding Lavanyavatee, the delight of his heart, exclaimed,—Dear Lavanyavatee! whither art thou going? Saying this, he got up from his seat, and, quite forgetful who was present, began to embrace her; whilst Charudanta, the miserable husband, stood gazing at her, motionless as a statue. And thus was a fool, by his own contrivance, plunged into the greatest distress. Now, I fear lest a similar fate should befall thee, concluded the mouse.

Manthara having attended to what had been said by the mouse, in great fear cried out,—My friends, I must go for security into the water. Saying this, he marched away, and Hiranyaka and the rest followed him; but they had not gone far, before Manthara was seized by a certain sportsman, who chanced to be hunting about in that forest, and who, finding himself hungry and fatigued, immediately fastened his game to the end of his bow, and turned his face towards home. The deer, the crow, and the mouse were exceedingly sorry for this event; and Hiranyaka expressed his lamentations in these lines:

'Before I have attained the end of one trouble, boundless as the great ocean, still a second is ready to succeed! How many misfortunes come upon me for my faults!

'A friend, who is so by nature, is the gift of providence. Such unfeigned friendship is not extinguished, even in misfortunes.

'Men have not that confidence in their mothers, in their wives, sisters, brothers, nor in their own offsprings, as in one who is a friend in principle.'

In this manner having lamented the fate of the tortoise, the mouse continued, crying out,—Oh! how hard is my fate! in the following words:

'By me have been experienced, even here, as

the fruits of the state of existence, in some certain birth, the good and evil shut up in time, which are the seekings of the offsprings of our own works. *

'The body is compounded with disorders, the state of opulence with calamities, advantages with disadvantages! Thus everything is produced with a companion who shall destroy it.'

Having again pondered for a while, he exclaimed,

'By whom was constructed that jewel of a word, the monosyllable FRIEND, that dispeller of fear, the

* This verse is written in a kind of measure which they call *eendra-vajra* (the lightning of the God of the heavens). The curious may not dislike to see it in its original form; from which, and the verbal translation, he may judge of Sanskrit composition in general, and find an excuse for the quaintness of the translation in some parts:

> swa-karma-santana-veecheshteetanee
> *own-work-offspring-seekings*
> kala-'ntara-'vreetta-soobha-'soobhanee
> *time-within-shut-good-not-good*
> eehi-'va dreeshtanee mayi-va tanee
> *here even seen by me even those*
> janma-'ntaranee-'va dasa-'phalanee
> *birth-within as it were stage of life fruits.*

The first and second lines contain but one compound word each; for there is no sign of either case, gender, or number, till you get to the end, where there is the termination of the plural number in the neuter. This manner of writing, which is very common, is called *samasa* (throwing or placing together), and is a most happy mode for the Brahmans, who are the interpreters of the law.

harbinger of grief, and the confidential repository of our joys?'

But,

'A friend who is a pleasing collyrium to the eyes, the delight of the heart, and a vessel in which may be deposited both joy and sorrow, is hard to be found by a friend.

'All other friends, tainted with the lust of gain, are everywhere to be found in times of prosperity; and adversity is their touchstone.'

Hiranyaka having in this manner greatly lamented the fate of his friend, said to the deer Chitranga and the crow,—Let our efforts be exerted for the deliverance of Manthara, before the hunter departs from the forest. Let us, said they, be instructed in what we should do. Let Chitranga go near the water, said Hiranyaka, and feign himself senseless and dead, and let the crow appear as if he were pecking at him; when the hunter, spying a deer, and longing to taste of his flesh, will be overjoyed, and so laying the tortoise upon the ground, will run to secure him. In the meantime I will gnaw asunder the cords by which Manthara is confined. The deer and the crow did as they were instructed immediately. The hunter being thirsty, laid the tortoise upon the ground, and having drank some water, sat down in the shade of a tree, when he discovered the deer in the situation above described. He concluded that he had been killed by some sportsman, and pleased with his good fortune, went towards him with a knife in his hand. In the meantime Hiranyaka contrived to loosen the cords by which Manthara was held; who finding himself at liberty made haste into the water; whilst the deer seeing the huntsman approaching, started up and ran away. The huntsman then turned back, and repairing to the foot of the tree, and not finding the tortoise there, he began to reflect in this manner,—I have been served right, said he, for not having been more circumspect.

'He who forsaketh a certainty, and attendeth to an uncertainty, loseth both the certainty and the uncertainty together.'

So, having said this, he returned home disappointed by his own folly; and the tortoise with the rest remained together in mutual happiness.

The Rajah's sons then said,—We have all been greatly entertained; and now is completed what we first wished for. May every other of your Highness's inclinations, replied Vishnu-Sarma, be accomplished like this!

'May you, ye good! find friends in this world! May Lakshmee be for ever to be found! May princes, resting upon their particular duty, govern and protect the earth!

'May the conduct of those who act well afford pleasure to the mind! By words alone no one is great. May he on whose diadem is a crescent,* cause prosperity to the people of the earth!'

* Seeva, the god of good and evil destiny, who is represented with a crescent in the front of his crown.

CHAPTER II.

THE SEPARATION OF A FAVOURITE.

HAVING, sir, said the young princes, heard The Acquisition of a Friend, we are now anxious to be informed of what respects The Separation of a Favourite.

Attend then, answered Vishnu-Sarma, and you shall hear concerning the Separation of a Favourite, of which these lines are an introduction:

In a certain forest there subsisted a great and increasing friendship between a lion and a bull, which is destroyed by a cruel and very envious jackal.

How was this? demanded the Rajah's sons; and Vishnu-Sarma related the following story:

FABLE I.

ON the southern road is a city, by name Ratnavatee,* where used to dwell a merchant's son, who

* Rich in precious things. Probably the name was made for the occasion.

was called Varddhamana,* though possessed of abundant wealth, seeing others his relations very rich, his resolution was that his own greatness should still be increased. They say,

'Greatness doth not approach him who is for ever looking down; and all those who are looking high are growing poor.'†

Again:

'Even a man who hath murdered a Brahman is respectable, if he hath abundant wealth. He may be of a race like that of the moon,‡ still, if he be without riches, he will be despised.

'Lakshmee, as a young woman likes not an old husband, doth not like to take unto her one without energy, the idle, him who trusteth in fate alone, or the man who is become destitute by his own extravagance.

'Idleness, the worship of women, the being afflicted with disorder, a foolish partiality for one's own native place, discontentedness, and timidity, are six obstructions to greatness.'

* Growing great, rich, or opulent. This is the true name of that city and province in Bengal, which we commonly call Burdwan.

† Whether this be the literal meaning of the author, the translator is not certain; if it be, he is at a loss to interpret it to his own satisfaction. [Neither elated nor dejected, look straight at the work before you.—H. M.]

‡ The Hindoo genealogists mention two races from which they boast descent: *the Soorya-bangs*, and *the Chandra-vangs*; that is, *the race of the sun*, and *the race of the moon*.

It is also said,

'A man should try to obtain what he hath not; having obtained it he should keep it with care; what hath been preserved he should increase, and being increased he should give it away at places of holy visitation.

'He whose days are passed away without giving or enjoying, puffing like the bellows of a blacksmith, liveth but by breathing.'

From the endeavours of one who longeth for what he hath not got, resulteth the acquisition. Property which hath been acquired, not being taken care of, wasteth of itself. Riches which are not recruited, like a collyrium,* by ever so small an expenditure, are in time reduced to nothing; if they are not appropriated, they are useless.

'What hath he to do with wealth, who neither giveth nor enjoyeth? What hath he to do with strength, who doth not exert it against the foe? What hath he do with the holy law, who doth not practise virtue? What hath he to do with a soul, who doth not keep his passions in subjection?'

Again:

* Crude antimony, and sometimes lead ore, ground to an impalpable powder, which the people of India put into their eyes by means of a polished wire dipped therein. They fancy it clears the sight, and increases the lustre of the eye.

'Having beheld the decrease of a collyrium, and the collected heap of the white ant,* a man should spend his days, which are not to be retarded, in acts of charity and the study of virtue.

'By the fall of drops of water, by degrees, a pot is filled. Let this be an example for the acquisition of all knowledge, virtue, and riches.'

These were the cogitations of the merchant; who accordingly took two bulls, the one called Sang-jeevaka,† the other Nandana,‡ and having yoked them to a cart loaded with sundry precious articles, departed for Kasmeera,§ for the purpose of trade.

For,

'What is too great a load for those who have strength? What is distance to the indefatigable? What is a foreign country to those who have science? Who is a stranger to those who have the habit of speaking kindly?'

As they were going over the mountain which is called Sudurga,‖ Sang-jeevaka fell down and brake his knee; seeing which, Varddhamana meditated in this manner:

* These destructive insects raise cones of cemented earth of an astonishing magnitude. They are frequently seen in Bengal eight or ten feet high, and of a proportionate bulk.

† *Living together*, alluding to his being yoked.

‡ Rejoicing.

§ The province of Cashmere.

‖ Of very difficult ascent.

One acquainted with men and manners may exercise his endeavours here and there; but, after all, the fruit will be whatever is in the will of providence.'

But,

'Hesitation should be abandoned as the opponent of every action; whence, having forsaken hesitation, let success attend the performance.'

Having thus determined, Varddhamana quitting Sang-jeevaka, pursued his journey; and the poor bull by resting his whole weight upon three feet contrived to get up; for,

'The destined age of every one defendeth the vitals of one plunged into the water, fallen from a precipice, or bitten by a serpent.'

In a few days, by feeding well upon what was most agreeable to him, he grew plump and full of spirits; and as he wandered about through the tracks of the forest, he made a great bellowing. In this same forest there resided Pingalaka,* a lion, in the full enjoyment of the pleasures of a dominion acquired by the strength of his own arm; for it is said,

'There is no ceremony of anointing, or inauguration, performed by the other animals upon the lion.

* A word expressive of the colour of a lion.

To be head of the beasts is the natural right of him who subdueth the kingdom by his prowess.'

One day, the lion being thirsty, went to the river-side to drink of its waters; when, hearing the bellowing of Sang-jeevaka, a kind of noise he had never heard before, and which to him appeared as dreadful as the unseasonable roaring of a cloud,* he turned away without drinking, and went back to his abode trembling with fear; where he stood silently meditating what it could be. In this situation the Rajah having been discovered by two jackals of his council, Karattaka and Damanaka,† the latter said to the former,—How is this, my friend, that the lion, although thirsty, has not drunk his usual draught, and stays at home so dull and dejected? Friend Damanaka, replied Karattaka, in my opinion we ought not to serve this same Rajah any longer; and that being the case, for what purpose should we

* A few years since there happened one of these unseasonable claps of thunder, without the least warning, from a single cloud that had by no means the appearance of one of those which threaten thunder. The lightning being attracted by the obelisk erected in Calcutta to the memory of those who suffered in the black hole, its shaft was greatly damaged, and a large slab of marble, on which was the inscription, burst from the iron clamps which held it to the brickwork, and shattered to pieces.

† These are the original names which the Persians, and, after them, the Europeans have corrupted into Kalila and Damna. The former may signify *one who liveth a reproachful life*, and the latter, *one who chastiseth, correcteth, tameth*.

investigate his motions, when we have served him so many years and experienced nothing but trouble?

'See what is done in serving by those slaves who are covetous of wealth! And see also what liberty the body is deprived of by those fools!'

Again:

'Those who are the dependents of another suffer cold, and wind, and heat, and fatigue! A wise man with a portion of it could do penance and be happy.

'So far life is worth having: to possess a livelihood without constraint; for if those who dwell under the authority of others live, pray who are the dead?

'Work, go, fall, rise, speak, be silent! In this manner do the rich sport with those needy men, who are held by the grip of dependence!

'Fools for the sake of gain dress themselves, and dress themselves to become the implements of others!'

Here is another very particular picture of a servant:

'He humbleth himself to be exalted; for a living he expendeth his vitals; he suffereth pain to acquire ease. Who is there so great a fool, as he who serveth?

'If he is silent, he is stupid; if rich in words, an empty prattler; by patiently submitting, he is a coward; and if he will not suffer patiently, for the most part, he is not preferred.

'Seen on one side, he is, undoubtedly, sitting down; and if standing at a distance, he is not to be found. The duties of servitude are extremely profound, and impracticable, even to Yogees.'*

What thou proposest, my friend, said Damanaka, is by no means to be put in practice.

'How! are not the mighty lords to be diligently served by thee, who, without delay, gladly fulfil the desires of the heart?

'When do those without employ enjoy those elevated stations distinguished by the Chamara,† the white umbrella spread upon a lofty pole, the horse, the elephant, and the splendid litter?'‡

Notwithstanding all this, observed Karattaka, what have we to do with this affair?§ One should always avoid meddling with other folks' business. See what is said upon this occasion:

The man who will have to do in matters with which

* Such as by severe acts of penance, and a total abstraction, fancy themselves in unity with the Supreme Being.

† A kind of whisk made of the tail of a particular species of cow, and sometimes of peacocks' feathers, finely ornamented, used to chase the flies away. In the vulgar dialect of Hindostan this instrument is called *chowry*, which seems to be a corruption of the Sanskrit term.

‡ The palanquin, properly *palkee*.

§ The lion's returning from the river without drinking.

he hath no business, may be repulsed and sleep upon he ground; like the ape who drew out the wedge.

How was that? demanded Damanaka; and he related the following story:

FABLE II.

In the country which is called Magadha,* Subhadanta, a man of the Kayastha tribe,† had begun to build a theatre for an entertainment. One of the carpenters having with his saw cut some way through a piece of timber, put a wedge into the slit. A troop of apes coming that way in search of their usual food, one of them, as if directed by the wand of Time, took hold of that wedge with his two hands, and sitting down, his lower parts hung within the slit. At length, from the natural giddiness of his species, with great difficulty he drew out the wedge, so that the boards closing, what was between them was entirely destroyed, and he deprived of his life. Wherefore, I say,

The man who will, &c.

For all this, said Damanaka, the concerns of the

* Probably the ancient name of south Bahar.

† The scribes, commonly called *kayts*, of which class are most of those employed by the English, and other Europeans, in India, as writers and accountants, under the titles *Sircar*, *Bannian*, *Cranny*, &c., and they are particularly famous for grand and expensive entertainments in honour of their divinities, which are generally given in temporary theatres of sufficient capacity to contain many hundred spectators.

master should certainly be looked into, even by the servant. The prime minister, observed Karattaka, being employed in the superintendence of all affairs, let him do it. An inferior should, on no occasion, interfere with the department of another; for,

He who shall meddle with the department of another, out of zeal for the welfare of his master, may repent; like the ass who was punished for braying.

Damanaka inquired how that happened; and Karattaka recounted the following story:

FABLE III.

AT Varanasee * there lived a washerman,† whose name was Karphoora-patta.‡ Once upon a time, having spent the evening until it was very late in the agreeable company of a young woman, he went to bed fatigued, and slept soundly. In the meantime, a thief got in with an intention to rob the house. In the court there were an ass and a dog. The ass said to the dog, upon hearing the thief,—This is thy business; then why dost thou not get up, and by barking contrive to rouse thy master? What hast

* The city we call Benares, which is a corruption of the former. It is a compound of two words denoting the two rivulets which bound that ancient city.

† Washing is seldom performed by women in India, except as help-mates to their husbands.

‡ White-cloth.

thou to do with my department? replied the dog. Thou knowest full well how I watch and guard this house, and yet this master of ours doth not consider my merit; and I am even stinted in my allowance of provisions. Now, masters in general, without spying some fault in their servants, are not wont to shorten their allowance. Hear me, barbarian!* exclaimed the ass. The dog species, from their nature, are not to be touched. But learn once more what is the duty of a servant:

'Is he a servant, is he a friend, who hesitateth at the time of action? Should the business be ruined, could it be occasioned by a servant, or by a friend?'

The dog replied,—Hear me for a moment:

'Is he a master who, at a proper season, doth not consider his servants? Are not they who keep servants on all occasions to cherish them?'

Do they not also say,

'Dependents should have no interrupters in their meals, in their amusements, in the execution of their duty, in their religious ceremonies, nor in doing good for the sake of virtue.'

The ass in a rage exclaimed,—Villain! thou neglectest thy master's business. Be it so; but it is my duty to do something that shall wake him; for,

* The original word is *barbara*. This is curious.

'The sun should be worshipped on the back, the god of fire on the belly, a master in every way, and the world above without deceit.'

Having repeated these lines, he began to make a great noise by braying; so that the washerman was alarmed; but, although exceedingly drowsy, he got up and gave the ass a good beating with a large stick. I repeat, therefore, "He who shall meddle," &c.

Observe: Our employment is searching for game; then let us attend to our proper business. But now I have considered, I think there is not any occasion for our doing that to-day; for there is plenty of provisions for us, and some to spare.

Damanaka, displeased at this observation, exclaimed,—What! Dost thou serve his Highness, the Rajah, merely for the sake of food? This is very unwise; as is declared in these lines:

'By the wise the patronage of princes is sought to gain the assistance of friends, as well as aid against the treachery of enemies; for, who doth not simply fill his belly?'

They say,

'Let him live, in whom living many live. Doth not even the booby fill his belly with his bill?'

Observe:

'What man with five Poorans* is reduced to servitude? Who upon a paralıel with riches is not found by riches? †

'Mankind being by birth upon an equality, the state of servitude is reproachful. He who is not the first of his species, is counted among those who are dependents.'

It is said also,

'The difference which is between horses, elephants, and vehicles; wood, stone, and cloth; women, men, and water, is a very great difference.'

For,

'A dog having found a bone with a few sinews sticking about it, dirty, loathsome, and without a bit of meat upon it, is rendered exceedingly happy, although it be not sufficient to satisfy his hunger.'

Whilst,

'The lion permitteth the jackal to come near and escape, and killeth the elephant. Every man, although reduced to distress, longeth for fruit suitable to his strength.'

* The term pooran (literally *ancient*) is given to such Hindoo books as treat of creation in general, with the particular genealogy, and history of their gods and heroes of antiquity. But why the number *five* is chosen in this place is not easily to be explained.

† Which seems to signify, *who may not acquire wealth if he exerts himself?*

Observe the difference in the behaviour of him who serveth, and of him who is served:

'Shaking the tail, falling down at the feet, and, prostrated upon the ground, looking up at his face and stomach: all this the dog performeth to his master who feedeth him. But the noble elephant looketh boldly, and eateth not, unless he liketh, with a hundred kind entreaties.'

But,

'That life, although it endure but for a moment, which is celebrated by mankind, as being attended by knowledge, valour, and renown, is, by those who know it, alone distinguished by the name of life. A crow liveth a long time, and a raven eateth.'

For,

'How is that brute-like man distinguished from a beast, whose understanding is void of the power to discriminate between good and evil, who is destitute of the many benefits of the sacred records, and whose only inclination is the filling of his belly?'

But what have we, interrupted Karattaka, to do with these reflections; we, who are of little power, and not the principal? In a very short interval of time a minister may enjoy the principal station, or the reverse, replied Damanaka; for, they say,

'No one is, by nature, noble, respected of any one,

nor a wretch. His own actions conduct him either to wretchedness, or to the reverse.'

Again:

'As by repeated efforts, a stone is mounted upon the summit of a hill, and instantly thrown down; so may we ourselves, by our virtues and our vices, be elevated and cast down.'

But after all, observed Karattaka, what is it thou art speaking of? The curious story, replied Damanaka, of his Highness Pingalaka's returning without drinking, and staying at home. What! demanded Karattaka, art thou acquainted with it? Is there anything, said Damanaka, unknown to a wise man? It is said,

'A declared meaning is comprehended even by brutes: horses and elephants understand when they are told; but a wise man findeth out even what is not declared. The advantage to be derived from our senses is to conceive what is only signified by another.'

Then, I will now, through the opportunity given by his fears, turn the fault to my own advantage, with the superiority of wisdom; for,

'He is a wise man who knoweth, that his words should be suited to the occasion, his love to the worthiness of the object, and his anger according to his strength.'

Friend, said Karattaka, thou art unacquainted with the ways of service.

'He who entereth uncalled for, unquestioned speaketh much, and regardeth himself with satisfaction, to his prince appeareth one of a weak judgment.'

How am I therein ignorant of the ways of service, demanded Damanaka; for,

'Is there anything of its own nature beautiful or not beautiful? The beauty of a thing is even that by which it shineth *

'One of a sound judgment having pursued a man with those very qualities of which he is possessed, may presently lead him into his power.'

Again:

'Upon hearing, "Who is here?" he should answer, "I!—please to command." And he should execute the orders of his sovereign to the best of his abilities.'

It is said,

'Disobedience of orders to the sovereign, and disrespect to the Brahmans, is death without the application of a knife.'

Again:

'He who is steady in trifling matters, wise, like a

* This passage seems to imply, that beauty should be estimated by good qualities, rather than by outward show.

shadow constantly in attendance, and who being ordered may not hesitate, is a proper person to dwell in the court of a prince.'

Sometimes, observed Karattaka, thy master is displeased with thee for thy unseasonable intrusions. It is true, replied Damanaka; nevertheless, attendants must, unavoidably, make their appearance. They say,

'The non-commencement of anything, from the fear of offence, is the mark of a weak man. Who, brother, leaveth off eating entirely, from the dread of indigestion?'

Observe:

'The sovereign serveth the man who is near him, although destitute of learning, of no family, or without acquaintance. Princes often, like women and vines, twine about him who sitteth by his side.' *

Well, said Karattaka, if thou go there, what wilt thou say to his Highness? Attend, replied Damanaka: First of all I will find out whether he is attached to me, or not attached. What signs, demanded Karattaka, are there of such a discovery? I will tell thee, said Damanaka; the signs of attachment are,

* This seems to argue that princes are apt to serve sycophants, and the panders of their pleasures, in preference to good and learned men.

'Joy at discovering at a distance, great attention and respect in inquiries, commending qualifications in absence, and remembering in those things which are favourites.

'Such knowledge of attachment, even in a servant, is an addition to one's happiness. The marks of attachment, even to a fault, are an accumulation of virtues.

'A wise man may also discover these signs in those servants who are not attached: squandering of time in idleness, increasing of hopes, and destroying the fruit.'*

When I have made this discovery, I will declare what my purpose shall be. Karattaka then said,—Notwithstanding this, it doth not behove thee to speak until thou hast found a proper opportunity. For,

'Even Vrihaspati,† should he utter words unseasonably, would incur contempt for his understanding, and eternal disgrace.'

Do not be alarmed, my friend, cried Damanaka, I shall not speak unseasonably; for,

'In misfortune, in error, and when the time appointed for certain affairs is about to elapse, a

* Disappointing.

† Amongst other titles given to this divinity, is that of *Master of Language.*

servant, who hath his master's welfare at heart, ought to speak unasked.'

Indeed, if I were not to give my counsel whenever I find an occasion, my office of counsellor would be useless.

'The qualification by which a man earneth his bread, and for which he is celebrated in the world, should be nourished and improved.'*

Then, peace be with thee! for know that I am going, concluded Damanaka. And may success attend thy design! replied Karattaka.

Damanaka, accordingly, repaired into the presence of Pingalaka, with hesitation, as it were; but as he was discovered by the Rajah at some distance, he entered with great marks of respect, and having performed that mode of prostration which is called Ashttangapata,† he drew near; and the lion, stroking him with his right paw, the toes of which were distinguished by ornaments, accosted him in the following words, which were preceded by a great many compliments: It is long since I have seen you, sir!

Damanaka replied: I have not the least occasion to attend your divine feet; nevertheless, a servant

* This verse was translated partly from conjecture, the original being defective in several words.

† This expression literally means *falling down with eight members*, which is the most humble and respectful mode of approaching a great personage in India.

should indispensably attend the presence at proper times; and thence it is that I am now here.

'Those who are penetrated with the timid principles of their instructors, despise the speeches of those, when approaching the presence of the sovereign, by whom, in wars, Surabhi,* of ponderous form and tall, the earth everlastingly to be adored, hath been pierced by the fall of a hundred weapons.'

Another poet says:

'The man whose heart is tainted with fear, although profuse of speech, in the presence of the king, amongst learned men, or in the company of women well inclined for a husband, is a coward.'

There is a use for the most trifling implements; as is mentioned in these lines:

'Sovereigns, O prince, have occasion even for straws, and things to rub the teeth, or pick the ears; but how much more for an able speaker, and a dexterous obviator of difficulties?'

Perhaps my noble master suspects, that being oppressed with years, my understanding is lost; for,

'Those who are possessed of good or bad qualities are not sensible of it themselves. The good traveller

* This name is also given to the *cow of plenty*, and this is the first time the translator has seen it applied to the earth; but the earth may well be called the cow of plenty.

doth not perceive that the Kastoorika* hath any enjoyment of her precious perfume.'

Nevertheless,

'Although a gem may tumble at the feet, and a piece of glass be worn upon the head, yet, at the season of buying and selling, glass is glass, and gems are gems.

'It should not be suspected of a man, whose life hath been spent in noble deeds, that his reason is lost, when he is only involved in trouble. A fire may be overturned, but its flame will never descend.'

Please your divine Highness, the master should conduct himself with distinction; for,

'When the master passeth over all alike, without distinction, then the endeavours of those who are capable of exertion are entirely lost.

'There are, O Rajah, three degrees amongst mankind: the highest, the lowest, and the middling; and accordingly, they should be engaged in three degrees of employment.

'Servants and houses should be suited to the situation. A gem should not be placed at the feet. The same is to be understood of an able man.'

Thus:

'If a gem be discovered at the feet, which is

* The musk deer.

worthy to be worn in an ornament of gold, and it doth not complain,* and it doth not also appear with splendour, he who placed it there is to be spoken to.'

Observe:

'"This is a man of judgment, and attached; and this a giddy fellow, and undisciplined." The chief, who knoweth how to judge of servants in this manner, is well served.'

They say:

'A horse, a weapon, a book, a Veena,† a speech, and a man or woman, are, or are not, to be employed, when their merits have been examined.'

Again:

'What is to be done with a faithful servant who is without ability; or with an able man who is an opponent? It doth not behove thee, O Rajah, to despise either the one or the other.'

For,

'The attendants of a prince, because of his dis-

* In this expression the allegory seems to be carried too far.

† An instrument of the string kind, very much esteemed in India. It is constructed of a long piece of wood upon which a number of steel strings are strained, and which serves also for the finger-board, it being furnished with frets almost from one extremity to the other, with each end fixed horizontally upon the pole (if the expression be allowed) of a large pumpkin, or an oblate sphere of wood hollowed for the purpose.

respect, grow thoughtless; and by that example men of judgment forbear to go near him.

'When a kingdom is forsaken by its wise men, the administration ceaseth to be efficacious; and for want of good regulations, the whole nation sinketh without power to resist.'

Again:

'Mankind are for ever wont to respect him who is respected by the prince; for he who is in disgrace with the sovereign is disrepected by all.

'What wise men have declared proper, may be received even from a child. When the sun is invisible, how useful is the appearance of the lamp!'

We are your faithful servants, attached to your Highness's feet; and we have no other place of refuge.

It is good, replied Pingalaka; but what of all this, Damanaka? Thou hast been for a long time our head Mantri-putra; * whither, then, hast thou been wandering in pursuit of vulgar sayings? Thou art now even prime minister.

Damanaka then said.—May it please your divinity, I am about to propose a question: What was the reason your Highness, when oppressed with thirst,

* The literal meaning of this term is *Counsellor-son;* but the context leads one to conclude, that the lion means to say, he has been a long time the principal of those who are inferior to the prime minister.

refused to drink, and now remains at home in a state of amazement?

It is well spoken, answered Pingalaka. How pleasant it is to repose a secret in a place of confidence! I am about to tell thee. Attend! Know that this forest is infested by some beast, before unknown to us; wherefore it behoveth us to abandon it. Hast thou not heard a strange loud noise? To judge by his voice, the strength of this monster must be excessive!

Please your divinity, replied Damanaka, there is indeed great cause for apprehension. We too have heard the voice; but he is unworthy to be a minister who, in the first instance, adviseth either to quit the field or to fight. Besides, your Highness has now an opportunity to experience the use of your servants; for,

'By the touchstone of misfortune a man discovereth the quality of wife, relations, and servants; and of his own strength and judgment.'

It is good, replied the lion; but I am prevented by my great apprehensions.

Damanaka having considered what he should do, at length said,—What! dost thou speak to us about a total abdication of the enjoyment of thy dominions? I tell your Highness plainly, that as long as I live, I shall not be afraid; but it is necessary that the minds of Karattaka and the rest should be pacified also; for in times of necessity, it is difficult to assemble people together.

After that Karattaka and Damanaka together, having received their sovereign's gracious commission, promised to defeat the threatened danger, and departed accordingly.

As they were going along, Karattaka said to Damanaka,—Is the cause of apprehension possible to be defeated, or not possible? Till this has been determined, why did we, in promising to apply a remedy, accept of this great appointment? For it is said, that no one, unless he hath the power to perform, should accept of any one's commission, and, in particular, that of a king.

Observe,

'He is all-glorious, on whose pleasure fortune waiteth, in whose valour victory, and in whose anger death.

'The sovereign, although but a child, is not to be despised, but to be respected as a man; or as a mighty divinity, who presideth in human form.'

Damanaka, laughing, said,—Hold thy peace, friend; I am acquainted with the cause of this fear: it is only the bellowing of a bull, our proper food, as well as that of the lion. If this be the case, observed Karattaka, why were not his Highness's fears instantly appeased? If, replied Damanaka, they had been satisfied immediately, how would this great commission have been obtained? They say,

*The master should never be rendered free from apprehension by his servants; for a servant having quieted the fears of his master may experience the fate of Dadhikarna.**

How was that? demanded Karattaka; and Damanaka related the following story:

FABLE IV.

UPON the mountain Arbuda-sikhara, there was a lion, whose name was Mahavikrama,† the tips of whose mane a mouse was wont to gnaw, as he slept in his den. The noble beast, having discovered that his hair was bitten, was very much displeased; and as he was unable to catch the offender, who always slipped into his hole, he meditated what was best to be done; and having resolved, said he,

'Whoso hath a trifling enemy, who is not to be overcome by dint of valour, should employ against him a force of his own likeness.'

With a review of this saying, the lion repaired to the village, and by means of a piece of meat thrown

* Whose ears are the colour of curds: *white-ear.*
† Great courage.

into his hole, with some difficulty caught a cat, whose name was Dadhikarna. He carried him home, and the mouse for some time not venturing out for fear, the lion remained with his hair unnipped. At length, however, the mouse was so oppressed with hunger, that creeping about, he was caught and devoured by the cat. The lion now no longer hearing the noise of the mouse, thought he had no further occasion for the services of the cat, and so began to be sparing of his allowance; and, in consequence, poor puss pined away and died for want. Wherefore, I say,—" The master should never be rendered," &c.

After this Damanaka and Karattaka advanced towards the bull Sang-jeevaka; and Karattaka seated himself in state at the foot of a tree, whilst Damanaka addressed the bull in these words,—Friend bull, said he, he who is sitting there is appointed General for the protection of these forests, by Rajah Pingalaka. Then Karattaka gravely said,—Come here directly, or else retire at a distance from these woods, otherwise the fruits of thy disobedience will be painful. The poor bull, ignorant of the affairs of the country he was in, fearfully advanced towards Karattaka, and made him a profound reverence. It is said,

'Wisdom .s of more consequence than strength. The want of it is a state of misery. The Din·

dima* proclaimeth this, sounding, "The miserable are defeated."

Sang-jeevaka, with a loud voice, said,—What, O General, am I to do? And Karattaka replied,—If it be thy wish to remain in these forests, bow down to the dust of his Highness's feet. Give me thy word, that there is no danger, said Sang-jeevaka, and upon those terms I am ready to go. These suspicions, observed Karattaka, are unnecessary; for,

'The tempest never rooteth up the grass, which is feeble, humble, and shooteth not up on high; but exerteth its power even to distress the lofty trees; for the great use not their might, but upon the great.'

Saying this, leaving Sang-jeevaka at a little distance, they repaired unto the presence of the lion, by whom having been received with attention, they made their reverence, and sat down; and the Rajah was well pleased.—Know, your Highness, said Damanaka, we have seen this animal, and he is humbled; nevertheless, he is of amazing strength! According to your divine commands, he is desirous of visiting your Highness's feet, wherefore, arm yourself, and let him draw near; for,

* A small drum which it is supposed Seeva, the destroying angel, will sound on the last day, when all things shall be dissolved.

'The bank is penetrated by the waters, although protected by a charm ; friendship is broken by maliciousness, and a coward is to be overcome by words alone.'

By this it is seen that one should not be alarmed at a mere sound ; for, it is said,

It is not proper to be alarmed at a mere sound, when the cause of that sound is unknown. A poor woman obtaineth consequence for discovering the cause of a sound.

The lion asked how that was ; and Damanaka recounted the following story :

FABLE V.

BETWEEN the mountains Sree-parvata there is a city called Brahma-puree,* the inhabitants of which used to believe, that a certain giant, whom they called Ghantta-karna,† infested one of the adjacent hills. The fact was thus : A thief, as he was running away with a bell he had stolen, was overcome and devoured by a tiger ; and the bell falling from his hand having been picked up by some monkeys, every now and then they used to ring it. Now the people of the

* There are many places in India called by this name, which signifies the *city of God*.

† Bell-ear.

town finding that a man had been killed there, and at the same time hearing the bell, used to declare, that the giant Ghantta-karna being enraged, was devouring a man, and ringing his bell; so that the city was abandoned by all the principal inhabitants. At length, however, a certain poor woman having considered the subject, discovered that the bell was rung by the monkeys. She accordingly went to the Rajah, and said,—If, divine sir, I may expect a very great reward, I will engage to silence this Ghantta-karna. The Rajah was exceedingly well pleased, and gave her some money. So having displayed her consequence to the priesthood of the country, to the leaders of the army, and to all the rest of the people, she provided such fruits as she conceived the monkeys were fond of, and went into the wood; where strewing them about, they presently quitted the bell, and attached themselves to the fruit. The poor woman, in the meantime, took away the bell, and repaired to the city; where she became an object of adoration to its inhabitants. Wherefore, I say,

It is not proper to be afraid of a mere sound, &c.

Having concluded his story, Damanaka and Karattaka brought Sangjee-vaka, and introduced him to the lion; after whieh the bull resided in that forest in great good fellowsbip.

Some time after, a brother of the lion's, whose name was Stabdha-karna,* coming to see him, Pingalaka having entertained him, they went forth to hunt for prey. Upon their return, Sang-jeevaka asked the lion what was become of the flesh of the deer which had been killed that day; and the Rajah told him that Damanaka and Karattaka knew. Let it be understood, said Sang-jeevaka, whether there is or is not any. There is not, then, replied the lion, laughing. What! said Sang-jeevaka, has so much flesh been eaten by those two? Eaten, wasted, and given away, answered the lion; and this is what happens every day. How are such things transacted, demanded the bull, without the knowledge of your Highness? Why not? said the lion. Because it is not proper, observed the bull: for it is said,

'A servant should never do anything of himself, without having informed the sovereign his master; except it be what he may do to prevent a misfortune.'

Again:

'The minister should be like a Kamandalu,† in which there is deposited a vast collection. Of what use to a sovereign is a poor idle fool, or a mere empty hull?

* Stiff-ear.

† A dish which beggars collect their alms in.

For,

'He is the best minister who enricheth the State but a Kakinee.* The treasury is the vitals of him who hath a treasury.† The animal spirits are not the vitals of princes.

'For a man will not arrive at the state of being respected by any other means. When a man is destitute of riches, he is sometimes forsaken, even by his wife, and how much more by others!'

What great evils these are also in a State!

Observe:

'Great expenditures, and the want of inspection; so, unlawful accumulation, plundering, and a distant situation,‡ are called the evils of the treasury.

'The rich man spendeth like Visravana,§ who squandereth, according to his inclinations, his income immediately, without regard to its amount.'

Stabdha-karna, the Rajah's brother, having attended to these words of the bull, declared his sentiments as follows:

Hear me, brother; it is my opinion that these two, Karattaka and Damanaka, being employed in the

* A small coin of the value of twenty cowries (small shells).

† A sovereign.

‡ It means probably, that when princes are absent from the seat of government, their officers are apt to be too prodigal of their treasure.

§ One of the titles of the Hindoo god of riches.

superintendence of the affairs of peace and war, are improper persons to preside at the head of the treasury. I will just repeat what I myself have heard upon the subject of persons to be employed.

Attend then:

'A priest, a soldier, and a relation, are not proper to be employed at the head of affairs. The priest, even when the object for which he was engaged hath been completed, refuseth to resign.

'If a soldier be employed in an affair, he directly showeth his sword; and the relation, presuming upon his relationship, swalloweth up all the profits.

'If an old servant be appointed, he will be fearless, even in the commission of crimes; and, in despite of his master, he may quit his service without reproof.

'One who hath been useful, in offending, payeth no attention to his offence. He maketh his services a standard, under which to plunder and destroy.

'What minister is inattentive amongst riches? The man forceth himself to be attached; and from intimacy * he is for ever sure to behave with insolence and contempt.

'A minister is always incorrigible, when he shall be grown too great. It is a maxim of those who are esteemed perfect, that abundance is the perverter of reason.

* Or, *from acquaintance.*

'The man who thinketh of nothing but the acquisition of wealth, always devoureth the whole without reserve. The eagle and the vulture may serve a prince as examples of such a minister.

'Not taking the advantages which are found,* concealing the expenditure of things, inattention, want of judgment, and the being addicted to pleasures, are all faults in a minister.

'The collection of the revenues is the business of the officers; but a constant circumspection, the payment of stipends, and of the return for labour, are the duties of the sovereign.

'Until they are pressed, they will not disgorge the royal treasures they have embezzled; for the officers of revenue, for the most part, are a corrupt class.

'And the compulsive power of the sovereigns of the earth should be exerted repeatedly upon their officers; for will a piece of cloth, by being once squeezed, yield up all the water it may have imbibed?'

The whole of this advice, concluded the lion's brother, should be put in practice, as often as there is found occasion.

The Rajah then said,—It is even so, that these two are not always ready to obey my commands.

* Not collecting the king's revenues.

And that, replied his brother, is at no time becoming in them: for,

'A sovereign should not forgive those who disobey his commands, although they were his sons. Especially if it be to the hurt of the revenue, or relative to anything he may have fixed his heart upon.'

Particularly as it is declared,

'The Rajah should, like a father, protect his subjects from robbers, from the officers of government, from the common enemy, from the royal favourites, and from his own avarice.'

Brother, continued he, let my advice be followed: We have made our meal for to-day. Then let the bull, Sang-jeevaka, who eats nothing but grass and corn, be appointed to superintend the provisions.

After that, he being appointed accordingly, the lion and the bull passed their time together in great mutual kindness. But the two jackals, upon experiencing a relaxation in serving out the provisions to the officers and dependents, began to consult together what was to be done. It is an evil of our own seeking, said Damanaka, and it is not prope. to lament about a misfortune of one's own making.

I, for having touched Swarna-rekha; the barber's*

* *Marked with lines of gold.* There is some degree of mystery in this verse, which will vanish upon reading the fable.

wife, for having bound herself; the merchant, for having attempted to steal a jewel: all these suffered for their own faults.

How was this? demanded Karattaka; and Damanaka related the following stories:

FABLE VI.

IN the city which is called Kanchana-pura* there was a Rajah, whose name was Veera-vikrama.† Once upon a time, as his chief officer of justice was conducting a certain barber to the place of execution, one Kandarpa-ketu, who was a traveller, accompanied by a merchant, taking him by the skirt of his garment, cried out,—This man is not guilty! How so! said the king's officers; not guilty, sayest thou? Hear me! said he, and he immediately began to repeat these lines:—"Having touched Swarna-rekha," &c. What does this mean? demanded the officers; and the traveller recounted the following adventure:

The king of Singhala-dweepa,‡ whose name is Jeemoota-ketu,§ hath a son called Kandarpa-ketu,‖ and I am he. One day a boatman, who attended in the pleasure gardens, told me that, on the fourth

* The golden city.

† Possessing the courage of a hero.

‡ The island of Ceylon.

§ *Jeemoota* signifies a *cloud*, and *ketu* a *flag*.

‖ One of the titles of the Hindoo Cupid.

day of the moon, there was to be seen in the sea, which was near, under what had the appearance of the Kalpa-taru, or tree of thought, seated upon a silver sofa, ornamented with a fringe of precious gems, a certain nymph playing upon a Veena, as it were the goddess Lakshmee.* At the proper time I sent for the boatman, and getting into the boat, set sail for the appointed place; and there I beheld a damsel, with only one half of her body appearing above the surface of the water. In short, attracted by the beautifulness of her appearance, I gave a jump with intention to catch her; but failing, I laid hold of a branch of the tree of thought, and was immediately transported to her golden palace; where I found her waiting in an apartment of gold, seated upon a bed of the same materials, attended by Vidya-dharees.† I no sooner saw her, than, spying me at a distance, she addressed me with respect, and offered to be my bride, to which I consented with my eyes; and we were immediately united by that mode of marriage which is called Gandharva-vivaha.‡ Her name was

* The goddess of good fortune. But as Saraswatee is more properly the goddess of harmony, it is apprehended her name should here be substituted for that of Lakshmee, which probably is a mistake of the copyist, who, in general, is very ignorant, and often unacquainted with every part of the language but the character.

† Literally, *female holders of science.* They are always represented as beautiful attendants, and are said to be of divine origin.

‡ This kind of marriage requires nothing but the consent of the parties, and in ancient times was lawful.

Ratna-manjaree,* and she was the daughter of Kandarpa-kelee,† the king of the Vidya-dhara.‡ One day, as we were in private together, she said,—Husband, thou mayest enjoy everything which is here according to thy wish, except it be the beautiful Swarna-rekha, a certain Vidya-dharee, who is not to be touched of any one. Some time after this, at an entertainment, being in a merry mood, I was tempted to touch her, and for my presumption she spurned me with the sole of her foot; after which I found myself in this country; and, at length, travelling about in great distress, I chanced to discover this city, and having wandered about all day, I went to sleep at the house of a certain cowkeeper. This man, too, perceiving the season for the commission of crimes§ was approaching, prudently quitted the conversation of his friends, and came home, where he found his wife planning evil with another woman. So, having given her a good beating, he made her fast to a post, and went to sleep. About midnight, the other woman, who was the barber's wife, returning, said to the cowkeeper's wife,—Such a one, burning with the fire of separation, is ready to die for thee. Go, then, to speak to him, and return quickly; and in the mean-

* A string of jewels.

† The sport of love.

‡ The plural of Vidya-dhara, in the masculine gender.

§ Night.

time I will bind myself to the post, and stay till thou shalt come back. Things having been thus managed, it so fell out that the cowkeeper waked. Why dost thou not now go to see thy gallant, my dear? said he; to which no answer being made, he continued, saying,—Pray who has taught thee to be so proud, that thou wilt not deign to give me an answer? and, saying this, he got up in a great rage, cut off her nose, and lay himself down to sleep again. After a while, the cowkeeper's wife returning, asked her neighbour what news. What news! said she; look in my face, and see what news! The cowkeeper's wife now takes her place, and binds herself to the post as before; and the barber's took up her nose and repaired to her own house. In the morning early, when the barber was hunting about for his razor case, his wife said,—Here is a razor, putting one into his hand; but as it did not chance to please him, he threw it in a passion upon the ground; upon which his wife seized the occasion to cry out,—Oh! without the least provocation, he hath cut off my nose! And away she went to the officer of justice.

In the meantime, the cowkeeper's wife, being questioned by her husband, exclaimed,—Who, guilty wretch, thinkest thou, is able to disfigure one so innocent as I? The eight guardians of the universe* are acquainted with all my actions! Is it not said,

* Eight deities supposed to guard eight points of the heavens.

'The sun and moon, fire and air, heaven, earth, and water; the heart, and conscience; day and night, with morning and evening; justice and all, are witnesses of a man's actions?'

Then, let this be the trial of my innocence:

'Ye mighty angels who guard the universe!' if I am an innocent wife, let this my countenance remain no longer without a nose!'

Now, said she, look at my face! Accordingly, her husband, having brought a light, examined her face; and when he beheld that it was free from any appearance of having been wounded, he fell down at her feet, and, with a joyful heart, released her from her confinement, and put her into bed. And now I have laid before you all this, I cannot help meditating upon the circumstance of the barber's wife having bound herself; but,

'Every book of knowledge which is known to Usana,* or to Vrihaspati, is by nature in the understandings of women.

'Honey dwelleth upon a woman's speech; but in her breast there is nothing but poison.'

Now attend to the history of the merchant: He left his own house, and after an absence of twelve

* The planet Venus, and the tutor of the evil spirits.

years, he returned to this city, having brought with him, from Manasotkantha,* a great many jewels, and went to sleep at a house. The mistress of the house had made a wooden image of a certain spirit, on whose head she had placed a valuable gem. This being told to the merchant, instigated by avarice, he got up in the middle of the night; but just as he had put his hand to the jewel, he was caught between the arms of the image, which were hung by wires, and squeezed very closely, so that he cried out with pain. The mistress of the house got up immediately. Ho, ho! master merchant! Thou art come from Manasotkantha! Then deliver all thy jewels, or else thou wilt not be released from thy present confinement. In short, he was helpless, and so sent for all his treasures, and made an offering of them for his enlargement; since which, having been thus plundered of all his wealth, he has joined our party of pilgrims.

The traveller having thus concluded the story of the merchant, the officers of justice released the poor barber. I repeat, therefore,—"I for having touched the damsel Swarna-rekha," &c. Now, continued Damanaka, as this also is an evil of our own seeking, it does not become us to grieve about it. And having considered for a moment, he added,—Friend,

* Probably the mines of Golconda.

the friendship which subsists between them was brought about by me; and, by me, that friendship may be dissolved; for,

'Skilful men make falsehood look like truth; and those acquainted with the painter's art, make an even surface appear uneven.'

The understanding which, upon unexpected occurrences, remaineth unaffected, may pass through the greatest difficulties; like the farmer's wife with her two gallants.

How was that? demanded Karattaka; and Damanaka recounted the following story:

FABLE VII.

AT a place called Dwaravatee,* a certain farmer had a beautiful wife, who used to keep company with the son of the magistrate of the place; according to these sayings:

'The fire is never satisfied with the addition of fuel, the ocean with the influx of rivers, the angel of death with the mortality of all things which have life, nor a beautiful woman with the conquest of all mankind!

'Women are never to be rendered faithful and

* One of the names of the place commonly called Dwaraka.

obedient; no, not by gifts, nor by honours, nor by sincerity, nor by services, nor by severity, nor by precepts!

'Women will presently forsake a husband, who is possessed of every good quality; reputable, comely, good, obsequious, rich, and generous, to steal to the company of some wretch, who is destitute of every accomplishment and virtue!'

One day, as she stood playing with the magistrate's son, she happened to see his father coming towards them; upon which, hiding the young man in the barn, she began to amuse herself with the justice himself. In the meantime, however, the husband making his appearance, she hastily told the magistrate to take a stick in his hand, and depart in a hurry, and with his eyes flaming, as it were, with anger. This being done accordingly, the farmer came up to his wife, and asked her what had occasioned the justice to be there in such a passion. Why, said the artful woman, you must know, that, for some cause or other, he is angry with his son, who flying here for protection, I hid him in the barn; but the father coming, and not finding him, is gone away in a rage. Saying this, she conducted her young gallant from the barn, and introduced him to her husband; according to this saying:

'What women eat, we are told, is twofold; their

cunning fourfold; their perseverance sixfold; and their passions eightfold.'*

Wherefore, I repeat,—"The understanding," &c.

Be it so, replied Karattaka; but how will it be possible to dissolve the ingrafted friendship which subsists between them? Some artifice must be thought of, replied Damanaka, according to this saying:

That may be effected by stratagem, which could not be effected by strength. A female crow, by means of a golden chain, caused the death of a black serpent.

How was this brought about? demanded Karattaka; and Damanaka told the following story:

FABLE VIII.

THE female companion of a crow resided in a certain tree, where she had young ones; but they were all devoured by a black serpent, who concealed himself in the hollow of its trunk. Now, finding herself breeding again, she said to her mate,—My dear, let us abandon this tree; for we shall never be able to raise any of our offsprings, because of that vile black serpent; for, you know,

'A bad wife, a false friend, servants who give pert

* This may be the case in India, to which the observation is confined.

answers, and living in a house infested by serpents, is death, as it were, inevitable.'

My dear, replied the crow, thou shalt have no further cause to be alarmed. I have pardoned his offence again and again; but this time he shall be prevented. How, husband, said the female, wilt thou be able to contend with one so powerful? Never fear, answered her mate:

He who hath sense hath strength. Where hath he strength who wanteth judgment? See how a lion, when intoxicated with anger, was overcome by a rabbit.

How was that? demanded the female; and the crow related the following tale:

FABLE IX.

UPON the mountain Mandara,* there lived a lion, whose name was Durganta,† who was perpetually complying with the ordinance for animal immolation;‡ so that, at length, all the different species assembled, and, in a body, represented, that as by his present mode of proceeding, the forest would be cleared all at once; if it pleased his Highness, they would, each of them in his turn, provide him an animal for his daily food; and the lion gave his con-

* A fabulous mountain.

† Hard-to-go-near.

‡ The Hindoos still offer kids and young buffaloes in their sacrifices.

sent accordingly. So every beast delivered his stipulated provision, till at length, it coming to the rabbit's turn, he began to meditate in this manner:—Policy should be practised by him who would save his life; and I myself shall lose mine, if I do not take care. Suppose I lead him after another lion? Who knows how that may turn out for me? Then I will approach him slowly, as if fatigued. The lion, by this time, began to be very hungry; so, seeing the rabbit coming towards him, he called out in a great passion,—What is the reason thou comest so late? Please your Highness, said the rabbit, as I was coming along, I was forcibly detained by another of your species; but having given him my word, that I would return immediately, I came here to represent it to your Highness. Go quickly, said the lion in a rage, and show me where this vile wretch may be found! Accordingly, the rabbit conducted the lion to the brink of a deep well, where being arrived,—There, said the rabbit, look down and behold him; at the same time he pointed to the reflected image of the lion in the water; who, swelling with pride and resentment, leaped into the well, as he thought, upon his adversary; and thus put an end to his life. I repeat, therefore, "He who hath sense," &c.

I have attended, said the female, to all this; and now, do as thou shouldst do in this matter. Every day, observed the crow, the king's son comes to bathe in the adjacent river. I mean to take away a golden chain he wears, when he shall take it off, and to put it into the hole where the serpent is; and when those who shall be employed to hunt after it shall search for it in the hollow of the tree, and shall see a black serpent, they will presently destroy it. Some time after, when the king's son was bathing in the river, the crow executed his plan; and the people sent to look after the golden chain found it in the hole, and killed the serpent. Wherefore, I say, "That may be effected by stratagem," &c. If it be so, replied Karattaka, go, and may thy ways be prosperous!

Damanaka, accordingly, went into the presence of Pingalaka; and having respectfully bowed, he addressed him in these words:—Please your Highness, I am come upon an extraordinary piece of intelligence, which, in my opinion, is not auspicious; for,

'He who hath another's welfare at heart should, in cases of calamity, erring from the right path, or when time and opportunity are passing away, declare his wholesome counsel, even unasked.'

Again:

'The sovereign being a vessel for the distribution of happiness, and not for the execution of affairs, the minister who shall bring ruin upon the business of the State is a criminal.' *

* Literally, *is tainted with evil.*

They say, also, speaking of ministers:

'Cutting off the head, or forsaking life, is better than negligence, from the wicked lust of obtaining the station of the master.'

The lion then graciously asked him, what it was that he wished to represent; and Damanaka replied,—Please your Highness, this same Sang-jeevaka is not such a faithful servant to thee, but that he can speak disrespectfully of thy three powers in my presence; and I know he has even an inclination for the sovereignty. Upon hearing these words, the lion was greatly alarmed, and remained in silent astonishment; whilst Damanaka continued thus:—Your Highness, in dismissing all your ministers, and appointing this bull to the superintendence of all affairs, has committed a great error. It is said,

'When both the sovereign and the minister are very highly exalted, Sree* standeth tottering with both her legs. That female, by nature, being unable to support so great a load, is obliged to forsake one of the two.'

And again:

'When a ruler of the earth maketh one man the prime and only minister of his dominions, and weakly confideth in him, he becometh intoxicated with power,

* One of the names of Lakshmee, the goddess of good fortune.

and is banished for negligence. The desire of liberty maketh an impression in the breast of him who hath been expelled; and at length, with that wish of liberty, he meditateth the death of his sovereign.'

They say,

'It is best to tear up by the roots, a rotten tooth, a faithless servant, and a wicked minister.'

And that,

'The sovereign who shall make fortune depend upon the minister, will, upon an emergent occasion, be at a loss, like a blind man without a guide.'

Particularly as,

'A minister who is grown too great is never to be corrected; and men who are esteemed perfect have declared that exaltation is an intoxicater of the mind.'

The bull proceedeth in every affair according to his own inclinations; and your Highness knows what is said upon such an occasion:

'There is not that man in the world who doth not long for fortune; and who doth not look at another's wife, if beautiful and young, with a degree of desire to possess her.'

The lion having considered for a moment, replied,—'Tis well; but provided it be as thou representest, still I have a great regard for Sang-jeevaka; and observe, that

'He who is dear to one, is dear even in the very commission of a fault. When the materials of a house are burnt, upon whose fire falleth disgrace?'

Please your Highness, said Damanaka, that even should not be; but it is true, that

'The man on whom the sovereign placeth an extraordinary degree of regard is the favourite of fortune; whether he be a son, a minister, or a stranger.'

And please to observe,

'To the unkind the ruin of the worthy bringeth delight. Fortune delighteth to be where there is a babbler and a listener.' *

And thus a primitive servant is neglected, and a stranger promoted. They say,

'A prince should not, because of the offence of an old servant, entertain a stranger, lest, between them, dissensions be created in the State.'

Thy words, exclaimed the lion, fill me with astonishment! Didst thou not thyself quiet my apprehensions, and present him to me? How then, now he is promoted, can he meditate evil?

* Or, *where there is an eloquent speaker, and one learned in the divine law;* for the same words will bear either interpretation.

Please your Highness, said Damanaka,

'The wicked, even whilst receiving favours, incline to their natural dispositions, as a dog's tail, after every art of anointing and chafing, to its natural bend.

'A cur's tail may be warmed, and pressed, and bound round with ligatures, and, after a twelve years' labour bestowed upon it, still it will return to its natural form.'

Again:

'In gratifying the wishes of men of vicious principles, when shall we find improvement, happiness, and purity? If the tree be poisonous, the fruit is unwholesome, although sprinkled with the water of immortality.'

Wherefore, I say,

'He who doth not wish another's ruin, should, even unasked, speak to him for his good. This is a supreme duty, and the contrary is the opinion of bad men.'

For it is declared,

'He is kind, who guardeth another from misfortune; that is an action, which is free from impurity; she is a woman, who can command herself; he is a worthy person, who is much respected by good men; he is a minister, who doth not behave with insolence and pride; he is happy, who is forsaken by his passions; that is friendship, which is not feigned; he is a man, who doth not suffer his members and faculties to give him uneasiness.' *

But if when all the inconveniences respecting Sangjeevaka have been pointed out, your Highness does not abandon him, there is no blame in your servant. It is said,

'When a prince is attached to his inclinations, he neither counteth the business which should be done, nor his own benefit. He proceedeth at liberty, wherever his passions lead him, like an intoxicated elephant. At length, when puffed up with pride, he falleth into a profound melancholy, he throweth the blame upon his servants, and doth not discover his own misconduct.'

To all this the lion observed,—'Tis said,

'One should not lift the rod against our enemies upon the private information of another; but having, by ourselves, made inquiry, we may either punish or commend.'

They say also,

'To seize and punish, before due investigation, may tend to our own destruction. It is like rashly forcing one's hand into the mouth of a serpent.'

* The original of this long verse is written in a kind of measure called *sardoolaveekreereeta*, consisting of four lines of nineteen syllables each.

It speaks plainly; nevertheless, shall proclamation be made that Sang-jeevaka is guilty of death?

Damanaka, a little confounded at this, replied,—Please your Highness, not so by any means; for by such procedure a breach is produced in our secret council; and they say,

'Having sown the seed of secrecy, it should be properly guarded, and not in the least broken; for being broken, it will not prosper.'

But,

'Time drinketh up the essence of every great and noble action, which ought to be performed, and is delayed in the execution.'

This being the case, what hath been begun should certainly be prosecuted with the utmost vigour; for,

'The resolutions of counsel are like a timid warrior, who, although attended by all his troops, beareth not to stand long, for fear of being defeated by the enemy.'

But after all, if when his offence shall be proved, he should be pardoned, and still retained, it will be exceedingly improper; for,

'He who wisheth to keep a friend after he hath once offended, receiveth death, as the Aswataree the belly.*

* The translator must confess he is ignorant of what this alludes to. The *aswataree* is a kind of serpent.

'When a bad man is employed near one, whatever he doeth is unprofitable. The Sakunee and the Sakata* may here serve a prince for emblems of such an one.'

Let me understand, said the lion, what it is he may be able to do against us; and Damanaka replied in the following lines:

Not knowing the nature of a man's connections, how shall we discover what he is able to do? The sea was once got the better of by a simple partridge.†

How was that? demanded the lion; and Damanaka related the following story:

FABLE X.

ONCE upon a time, a female partridge, who resided upon the sea-shore, finding herself pregnant, said to her mate,—My dear, pray let a private place be sought convenient for me to be brought to bed in. Is not this where we are a proper place for that purpose? demanded the partridge. No, replied the female, because it is frequently overflowed by the tide. What! exclaimed the male, am I so much less powerful than the sea, that I should suffer myself to be insulted, even in my own house? My dear!

* The former signifies *a vulture*, and the latter is a bird unknown to the translator, and not described in any of his nomenclatures.

† In the fables attributed to Pilpay this bird is called Gerandi. The name in Sanskrit is Teeteebha.

replied the female, laughing, there is a great difference between thee and the sea; otherwise,

'He whose understanding can discern what is, and judge what should or should not be applied to prevent misfortune, never sinketh under difficulties.'

After this, however, and in obedience to the commands of her mate, she laid her eggs in the same place; and the sea, to try the power of the partridge, came and carried them off in triumph; whereupon, the poor female, overwhelmed with affliction, said to her husband,—O master of my heart, what a misfortune has befallen us! The sea has stolen all my eggs! My dear, replied the partridge, do not be alarmed; but wait and see what I am capable of doing. So, upon saying this, he assembled all the other birds, and having informed them of what had happened, one of them said,—We are not powerful enough to contend with the mighty ocean; but I recommend, that at a proper time we should go in a body, and represent the affair to the eagle,* who will ease us of our troubles. Having considered this proposal, they all repaired into the presence of the king of birds, and laid their grievance before him; who, having heard it, considered for a moment what he should do:—I will, said he to himself, state the case to the

* In the original Garootwanta, the bird of Vishnu, otherwise called Garoora.

great and mighty lord, Narayana, the author of creation, preservation, and destruction,* and he will wipe away our sorrows. Accordingly, the eagle, attended by the rest of the birds, addressed their complaint to Narayana, saying,—O Lord! Even whilst thou art master, the sea hath dared thus to overwhelm us! The deity having considered their complaint, commanded the ocean to surrender the eggs; and the king of waters placed the high decree upon his crown, and delivered up the eggs accordingly; and the birds having gained what they wanted, returned thanks, and retired to their own abodes. I repeat, therefore, "Not knowing," &c.

'The enemy who commenceth hostilities, without having considered the transgression of the law, meeteth a defeat, like the sea from the partridge.'

How shall we discover, said the lion, when the bull is maliciously inclined? Your Highness, replied Damanaka, will know when you shall behold him coming, with those weapons the tips of his horns pointed towards you, looking as if alarmed. Having said this, he went where Sang-jeevaka was; and being in sight of him, he advanced by slow degrees, and made himself appear as if agitated by something.

* Though this attribute more particularly belongs to Seeva, yet it is common to allow the same powers to each of the three persons of the Hindoo trinity, Brahma, Vishnu (or Narayana), and Seeva, seeing they mean but one God, Brahm or Brahma.

Health and happiness attend thee! said Sang-jeevaka, with great marks of politeness. Alas! replied Damanaka, where is there any happiness for those who are in a state of dependence? For,

'The fortunes of those who serve princes are in the power of others; their minds are never at ease; and they have no confidence even in their own lives!'

Again:

'Who, having obtained riches, is not proud? From whose misfortunes do the luxurious become so? Whose heart hath not been tormented by women? Or who is dear to a king? Who is there not within the arms of time? What beggar ever arriveth at consequence? Or what man who hath fallen into the snares of the wicked hath escaped in peace?'

Pray, friend, said the bull, inform me what all this means! Oh! my friend, replied he, what shall I say, but that I am very unfortunate!

'I am now like one plunged in a deep water calling out for help, who findeth many things hanging down to assist him, which he neither quitteth nor taketh hold of.

'Confidence in the prince, all at once, ruineth one friend or other! What shall I do? Whither shall I go? I am fallen into a sea of trouble!'

Having said this, he heaved a deep sigh, and sat

down; then Sang-jeevaka desired him to relate, more fully, the cause of his uneasiness; and Damanaka with great show of secrecy said,—Although it be highly improper to abuse the confidence of one's sovereign, yet, as it was at our instance thou camest, it behoveth me, as I hope for welfare myself hereafter, to inform thee of what concerns thy own welfare. Attend then:—His Highness is very much enraged against thee, and has declared in private, that he will have Sang-jeevaka killed; and that he will treat his attendants with his flesh. The bull, upon hearing this, became very sorrowful; whilst the artful Damanaka cried,—It is in vain to be melancholy; rather let something be pursued suitable to the occasion. Sang-jeevaka was thoughtful for a moment, and then calmly said,—These lines are uttered from a pious mouth:

'Unworthy to be found by bad men, sovereigns, for the most part, are cherishers of the undeserving. Riches are attendants of the miser; and the heavens rain plenteously upon the mountains!'

What is my own opinion? I know not! nor is this an affair to be discovered.

'The unfortunate man who possesseth splendour from the glory of him on whom he dependeth, will find it as fatal as a foul collyrium put into the eye by the hand of imprudence.'

But when I reflect, how hard is the sentence which hath been pronounced against me!

'The king hath been courted with unremitting pains; why then is he not pleased? Herein is the wonder! This too is a circumstance before unparalleled: one whilst he is served is about to be an enemy!'

Then, this may be deemed something inexplicable; but,

'The man who, having discovered some unfavourable token, giveth way to his passions, will certainly fail in the pursuit of it. How shall one give satisfaction to him whose mind is displeased without a cause?'

Have I offended the king by taking grain; or are princes apt to become enemies without sufficient cause?

Damanaka replied,—Thus it is! Hear me:

'Some are discontented, even with the assistance of the whole body of able men; whilst others are pleased when offences are committed in their sight. The duties of servitude are exceedingly profound: they are impracticable, even to those who are in the habit of doing penance; because those who are not servants for one thing alone, must submit to be directed by the eye at the sovereign's will.'

Again:

'Virtues amongst those who know what virtues are, are virtues; but when they meet with a subject destitute of good qualities itself, they become faults.* Rivers flow with sweet waters; but having joined the ocean, they become undrinkable.

'A hundred good actions are lost upon the unworthy; a hundred fine speeches are lost upon the ignorant; a hundred good qualities are lost amongst men who are destitute of good qualities; a hundred times speaking is lost upon those who are not inclined to converse; a hundred understandings are lost upon the insensible.' †

It is true, replied the bull, that

'Serpents are found upon the sanders tree; in the waters the lotus flowers with alligators; and in the midst of full enjoyment those who dispute about the quality.' ‡

Away then with uninterrupted happiness!

'If the deserts were made liquid, and the waters

* Does so much of this verse mean that good qualities are lost upon bad men: are despised by them, or that virtue is corrupted by bad company?

† It is hard to determine what the author intended by this sentence, unless by the word rendered *understandings* he meant *wise judgments*, *sensible observations*.

‡ By the context this should mean, that we find cause to complain, even in the midst of fruition, there being no such thing as perfect happiness.

rendered solid; I ask if the former might not be passed in boats, and the latter be called dry land.*

'He who serveth an unreasonable man, acteth as much in vain, as he who soundeth a trumpet in the ears of the deaf, or presenteth a mirror to the blind.

'The root is infested by serpents, the flowers by bees, the branches by monkeys, and the leaves by insects; in short, there is not a sanders tree which is not surrounded by the vilest impurities.'‡

Our master, observed Damanaka, is one of those who carry honey in their speech, and poison in their hearts; according to this description:

'He holdeth out his hands at a distance;§ he appeareth with a wet eye; he relinquisheth one half of his seat; he is fond of close embracing; his words in conversing are kind and gentle; he bestoweth compliments; his inside is naught but poison, whilst without he is covered with sweets; and he is rich in extreme deceit. What name is there for this before unheard-of mimic art, which is inculcated by wicked men?'

It is said,

* This verse, as connected with that which immediately precedes it, seems to imply that unsullied happiness must not be expected till the order of nature be reversed.

† The Hindoos seem to have been long acquainted with the art of constructing mirrors of polished plates of steel.

‡ This verse seems to have been misplaced.

§ In the attitude of invitation; joined, with the palms upwards.

'The boat was invented upon crossing pieces of water which were difficult to pass; the lamp, upon the approach of darkness; the fan, upon a defect of wind; and injuries, to gratify the pride of men blinded by intoxication! In short, there is not anything in the world, wherein the idea of invention was not suggested by Providence.* But, in my opinion, Providence itself would fail in its endeavours to prevent what passeth in the minds of wicked men.'†

How hard it is, exclaimed Sang-jeevaka, that this poor feeder upon grass and grain, should be an object worthy to be ruined by a lion!

'The disputes of two of equal strength and fortune are worthy of attention; but not of two, the one great, the other humble.

'What animal, being athirst, from its clearness willingly attempteth to enter the sun when standing upon the summit of the western mountains? The bee flyeth to the lotus.‡

* The original word is ambiguous, and might, with equal propriety, have been interpreted by the term *chance.*

† The length of this verse in English, when compared with its original, is twofold, the latter containing only four lines of nineteen syllables each; but as it is hardly possible to express the same idea clearly in our language with fewer words, this remark may serve to show that the Sanskrit cannot be rendered intelligible in the dialects of Europe, but by a periphrasis.

‡ This verse is rather darkly expressed. As connected with what precedes it, it may argue that, in general, animals though ever so much pressed by their passions or appetites, are not wont to attack such as are stronger than themselves.

'Exulting with the rage of madness he springeth upon the noble elephant; or else, having quitted him without pity, he is engaged by his people amongst vagabonds.*

'The tree is broken down by the abundance of its fruit, and walking groweth tiresome to Sikhandis.†

'The minister is like a beast of burthen, who is led by sweet words. Good qualities in a virtuous person, for the most part, are his enemies.‡

'Princes, in general, alas! turn away their faces from a man endued with good qualities. Women, too, often delight in those who are fond of delight. This is a false position, that virtue leadeth to the society of men; for mankind, generally, do not reckon this a noble principle.' §

It is well! continued Sang-jeevaka, addressing himself to Damanaka, this poor attendant is of no esteem with the Rajah!

* This verse is deficient in the original. The meaning of it, as far as one can judge from what remains, seems to be that tyrants are either engaged in cruel wars, or else, under the influence of parasites, spending their time at home in idle pleasures, which is but too common with the princes of Hindostan.

† This word probably signifies *peacocks*. The intention of the verse seems to be this,—that wealth and greatness are frequently the ruin of those who possess them. The peacock is famous for running fast, but his superior agility soon fatigues him.

‡ From the latter part of this verse the former should signify that the minister who yieldeth to the opinion of his sovereign, though destitute of every good quality, is the most likely to be a favourite.

§ This verse, in the original, is full of blunders. The translator thinks his version is according to the author's meaning.

'It is better that the vulture should be followed by geese, as ministers and attendants; than that the goose should be pursued by the birds of prey which attend the offerings made to the manes of the dead. An attendant being angry may use even a hundred harsh expressions; but a virtuous man is not to be deprived of any of his good qualities by his feeble assistants.' *

The bull having again considered a while, continued saying,—I know not by what fault of mine the Rajah has been injured, that he should be at variance with me! It is best therefore to be for ever jealous of a prince.

'If ever the mind of a king, which is like a bracelet of solid crystal, is injured by his minister, who is the artist that can repair it? †

'A thunderbolt, and the power of kings, are both dreadful! But the former expendeth its fury at once, whilst the latter is constantly falling upon our heads.'

Having pondered for a while, he said to Damanaka, —It behoveth thee, my dear friend, to afford me such

* The first period ending with the word *dead*, as applicable to the subject, seems to imply that the poor bull, who was the lion's minister, being by nature much weaker than he, his master had no real cause to be apprehensive of danger from him. This makes a distinct verse in the original, and was joined to the next period, which is also a complete verse, by mistake.

† Does the author of this verse mean that offended princes are not easily pacified?

advice on this fatal occasion, as the nature of the case seems to demand. What hath been the practice of many, flourisheth in misfortune. Although it be as thou observest, replied Damanaka, yet those acquainted with the rules of prudence say,—"The loss of one's own life," &c.* May this happen to me, exclaimed Sang-jeevaka, in the field of battle; for death would, in my mind, be preferable to the imputation of fear. At present that doctrine † is not suitable.

'Or dying, he obtaineth heaven; or having killed his enemy, the enjoyments of life. Both these hard-to-be-acquired blessings are the rights of heroes.

'As out of battle death is certain, and in the field life doubtful, the learned call it "the only time of battle." ‡

'When out of battle he beholdeth no happiness for himself, the wise man embraceth death fighting the foe.

'In victory he obtaineth fortune, and in death celestial beauty. Seeing that our bodies are so very fragile, why should we hesitate about dying in the battle?'

Let me clearly understand, my friend, how I am to discover when he is determined to put me to death.

* A partial quotation of some well-known maxim.

† Probably the doctrine laid down in the above partial quotation.

‡ Dying sword in hand.

F 2

When the Rajah shall cock his tail, lift up his paws, and look at thee with his mouth open, replied Damanaka, then will be the time for thee also to display thy prowess.

'Strong even without vigour, who may not experience the situation of being defeated? Observe how fearlessly people put their feet upon a heap of ashes!'

But it is necessary that everything be conducted with the greatest privacy. Having said this, Damanaka went to join Karattaka; who asked him what was effected. Why, replied the former, a reciprocal breach hath been effected between the two. What doubt of it? cried Karattaka; for they say,

'What a name is relation amongst wicked men? Who will not be angry when over and above solicited? Who groweth satisfied with riches? Who, being attentive, may not be learned?'

Likewise:

'A man is rendered miserable by artful people, and prosperous from the greatness of his soul. What, doth not a troop of villains act, like the fire (whose epithet is destroyer of that which is intrusted to him?)'

After this Damanaka went to the lion, and cried out,—Please your Highness, that vessel of iniquity is coming! Prepare thyself, and let him approach! Having said this, he caused the lion to put himself in the attitude before described; and Sang-jeevaka being arrived, upon seeing the lion with his countenance thus altered, began himself to display a corresponding show of defiance. At length there ensued a furious battle, in which the poor bull having been killed by the lion, the latter overcome with fatigue, and standing, as it were, full of affliction, exclaimed,— Alas! what a cruel action have I been guilty of!

'If the dominion be enjoyed by others, he himself is the vessel which containeth the fault. Should a prince transgress the law, he is like the lion after the murder of the elephant.*

'The loss of territory, or of a wise and virtuous servant, is a great loss. The loss of servants is death to sovereigns, and the loss of empire; for servants are not easily to be found.'†

What novelty is this? cried Damanaka. It is very unusual for one to lament having put a faithless enemy to death; and indeed it is very improper to do so.

'Or father, or if a brother; or son, or if a friend,

* The translator must confess he is ignorant of what this sentence alludes to.

† That is, good servants.

be a conspirator against his life, he should be put to death by a prince who wisheth his own welfare.

'One acquainted with the principles of justice and political interest, should neither be hastily severe; nor ever ready to pardon, although money be in the hand. It is proper to swallow mercy.

'It is a virtue in hermits to forgive their enemies, as well as their friends; but it is a fault in princes to show clemency towards those who are guilty.

'There is no other but one expiation for him who, from pride and the lust of power, shall wish for his master's station, and that is death!

'A meek-hearted prince, a Brahman who eateth of all things alike,* an unruly wife, a bad-principled companion, an unfaithful servant, and a presumptuous superintendent, should all be put away: they are not worthy to be tried seven times.'

But the following lines give a very particular picture of the behaviour of princes:

'The conduct of princes, like a fine harlot, is of many colours: true and false; harsh and gentle; cruel and merciful; niggardly and generous; extravagant in expense, and solicitous of the influx of abundant wealth and treasure.'

* Although the Brahmans are by no means confined to a vegetable diet, as is generally supposed, still, like the Jews and Mussulmans, they are forbidden to taste of many kinds of flesh and fish.

The lion having been thus composed by the arts of Damanaka, at length recovered his natural temper of mind, and seated himself on his throne; and Damanaka, with his heart full of exultation, having wished victory to the mighty king, and happiness to all the world, lived ever after according to his wish.

Vishnu-Sarma, having thus concluded his second head, The Separation of a Favourite, gave notice to the young princes; who declaring they were well pleased with it, he gave them his blessing and repeated the following lines:

'May such a breach between friends happen but in the house of your enemies! May traitors, day by day, be led by Time to their destruction! May the people be perpetual possessors of abundance, and all the blessings of life! And may youth for ever find amusement here in this pleasant garden of fable!

CHAPTER III.

OF DISPUTING.

THE time set apart for hearing these stories being arrived, the young princes reminded Vishnu-Sarma in these words:—Worthy sir! As we are the sons of a prince, it will afford us very great amusement to hear what relates to Disputing. And Vishnu-Sarma replied,—If it will give you pleasure, I will proceed to recount what is connected with that head, to which the following verse is the introduction:

In a quarrel between the geese and the peacocks, in which is displayed equal valour; the geese, having trusted them, are betrayed by the crows who were in the camp of the enemy.

How was this? demanded the young princes; and Vishnu-Sarma related as follows:

FABLE I.

IN Karpura-dweepa* there is a famous lake which

* *Karpoora* signifies *camphire, gold,* and a particular tree commonly called *plas;* and *dweepa,* an island. The translator is ignorant of the situation.

is distinguished by the name of the Padma-nilaya,* where used to reside a royal goose, whose title was Hiranya-Garbha,† and who had been appointed their king by all the birds who are wont to frequent the waters.

'If there were no king, the people would thence be entirely ruined; they would be here like a boat in the water without a pilot.

'The king protecteth the people; and they support the greatness of their sovereign. But protection is better than greatness; for the one cannot exist without the other.'

One day as the royal goose was sitting upon a bed of lotus flowers finely spread, surrounded by his attendants, there arrived from some distant country a certain booby, whose name was Deergha-mukha, who, having made his obeisance, drew near. Deergha-mukha! said the king, thou art lately come from foreign countries: pray inform me what news. Please your Highness, replied the booby, I have some very important news, anxious to relate which I made haste to come here. In Jambu-dweepa,‡ there is a

* Lotus-habitation.

† Gold-belly.

‡ The habitable part of the earth, according to the ancient Hindoo geographers. Almost every preceding author has declared that this name is derived from two words, the former signifying *a jackal*, and the latter *an island* or *continent*, into which error they have been led by the

mountain called Vindhya, where reigns Chitra-varna,* a peacock, who is there king of the winged tribes. As I was walking one day over a place where the grass and underwood had been burnt down, I was discovered by some of his attendants who were passing by; and upon their asking who I was, and whence I came, I replied, that I came from Karpura-dweepa, that I was an attendant of the royal goose, king Hiranya-Garbha, and that I came there out of curiosity to see foreign countries. They then asked me which of these two countries I thought the best; and I said,—O what a question is this! There is a vast difference between them: Karpura-dweepa is a heaven of a place! Then what do you do in such a barren country as this? Come away, and accompany me into our country. But upon hearing me talk in this manner, they seemed to be very much displeased. They say,

'A draught of milk to serpents doth nothing but increase their poison. Good counsel bestowed upon fools doth rather provoke, than satisfy them.

affinity of the word Jamboo to Jambooka, this last signifying a jackal; but the truth, according to the authority of Sanskrit dictionaries and a definition found in an original work treating of that country, is that Jamboo is the name of a tree which bears a fruit commonly called *zamin* or *jamin* in Hindostan. The Hindoo poets have imagined that in the centre of this *dweepa* (island or continent) there was a tree of that species of an amazing size, whence it derived the name of Jamboo-dweepa.

* Motley-colour.

A wise man is worthy to be advised; but an ignorant one never. Certain birds, having given advice to a troop of monkeys, have their nests torn to pieces, and are obliged to fly away.*

The royal goose demanded to know how that was; and the booby repeated the following story:

FABLE II.

ON the banks of the river Narmada,† upon a neighbouring mountain, there was a large Salmalee tree, wherein certain birds were wont to build their nests and reside, even during the season of the rains. One day, the sky being overcast with a troop of thick dark clouds, there fell a shower of rain in very large streams. The birds seeing a troop of monkeys at the foot of the tree, all wet, and shivering with cold, called out to them,—Ho, monkeys! why don't you invent something to protect you from the rain?

'We build ourselves nests with straws collected with nothing else but our bills. How is this, that you, who are blessed with hands and feet, yield to such sufferings?'

* When the learned Pandit, under whom the translator studied the Sanskrit language at their holy city of Benares, used to be reproached by other Brahmans for communicating the key of their divine mysteries to foreigners, he constantly silenced them by repeating this hemistich in the original.

† A river which empties itself into the Gulf of Cambay, commonly called the Narbada.

The monkeys hearing this, and understanding it as a kind of reproach, were exceedingly irritated, and said amongst themselves,—Those birds there, sitting comfortably out of the wind within their warm nests, are laughing at us! So let them, as long as the shower may last. In short, as soon as the rain subsided, the whole troop of them mounted into the tree, where tearing all the nests to pieces, the eggs fell upon the ground and were broken. I say, therefore, "A wise man is worthy to be advised," &c.

Well, said the royal goose, what did the birds say after they had heard this story? Why, please your Highness, they were in a great passion, and asked, who made that same goose a king! In answer to which, I too, in the anger which such a question created, cried,—By whom was this same peacock made a king? and, upon my saying this, they tried to kill me, and in return, I displayed no little valour.

'An occasional dress to a man is as forgiveness and modesty to a woman. Courage when surrounded is like being captive amongst men endued with clemency.'*

The royal goose smiling at this, said,

'A man who, having well compared his own strength or weakness with that of others, after all,

* This verse wants precision, but the intention is clearly this: that an assumed character may sometimes serve one, instead of a real one.

doth not know the difference, is easily overcome by his enemies.'

A fool is always discovered if he stayeth too long; like the ass dressed in a tiger's skin, from his voice.

How was this? said the booby; and the royal goose related the following tale:

FABLE III.

AT Hastinapura* there lived a certain dyer, whose name was Vilasa.† He had a jackass who was grown exceedingly weak by carrying burdens too great for his strength, and, as it were, almost at the point of death. In this condition the dyer dressed him up in a tiger's skin, and let him loose in a field of corn; so that the people belonging to the field having observed him at a distance, ran away with the idea of its being a real tiger. After a while, however, a man whose business was to watch the field, having dressed himself in a kind of armour made of an ass's skin, and furnished himself with a bow and arrows, ventured to approach him; and the supposed tiger, who was now grown plump and fat, spying him at a little distance, and thinking it was a female of his own species, began to welcome her by setting up a loud braying, and immediately trotting up before her.

* The ancient name of the city of Delhi.

† Artful.

But the man having discovered from his voice what he really was, the poor ass was soon overcome for his love. I say, therefore, "A fool is always discovered," &c.

After that, said the booby, the birds called out to me,—Rascal! vile booby! Dost thou dare speak thus slightingly of our sovereign? This is not to be suffered by us presently! And, saying this, they began to attack me with their bills, and to brave me in this manner:—Observe, thou stupid animal! thy goose is always a soft spiritless creature; although he is by no means so very mild in the government of his dominions; but he is incapable of possessing as much wealth as would lie in the palm of one's hand; how then shall he command the universe? As for thyself, thou art like an angry frog; but he is thy superior. Hear this:

'A large tree, which yieldeth both fruit and shade, is highly to be esteemed; but if Providence, perchance, may have denied it fruit, by whom is its shade refused?' *

And, that

'Court should not be paid to the indigent; but to him on whom there is great dependence. The

* This verse, which is certainly a beautiful one, as quoted by the subjects of the peacock, can only be applicable to him.

elephant obtained the title of Varunee from his carrying water in his trunk. For,

'Even the greatest are reduced to littleness, and those of abundant qualities to insignificance, by the properties of that by which they are opposed; like the royal elephant in the mirror.'

Besides,

Great things may be effected by wise counsel, when a sovereign enemy may be too powerful. Certain rabbits were enabled to live in comfort, through the policy of one of their brethren.

I asked them how this was? And the birds related as follows:

FABLE IV.

ONCE upon a time, for want of rain in due season, a troop of elephants being greatly distressed for water, addressed their chief in these words:—What resource have we, except in that hollow sinking ground inhabited by those little animals! but deprived of that too, whither, sir, blinded as it were, shall we go? What shall we do? Upon hearing their complaints, their chief, after travelling with them a great way, discovered a fountain of clear water. But as many rabbits who happened to be in their

* A derivation from Varuna, the Hindoo Neptune.

burrows were crushed to death under the feet of so many elephants trampling over their warren; at length, one of them, who was called Silee-Mukha,* reflected in this manner:—This troop of elephants, oppressed with thirst, will be coming here every day to drink, and, at length, our whole race will be destroyed! But an old buck, whose name was Vijaya,† said to him,—Brother, don't be uneasy; for I am going to prevent what thou dreadest. Saying which, he set off to try how he could oppose them; but as he went along, he began to consider how he should approach so formidable a troop; for, observed he, they say,

'An elephant killeth even by touching, a serpent even by smelling, a king even by ruling, and a wicked man by laughing at one.'

Wherefore, I will mount the summit of a rock to address the head of the troop. This being put in execution accordingly, the chief elephant asked him who he was, and whence he came. I am, he replied, an ambassador sent here by the god Chandra.‡ Declare the purport of thy commission, said the elephant. Sir, replied the rabbit, as

* This name seems to imply *a blockhead.*
† Victory.
‡ The moon, which is esteemed of the masculine gender by the Hindoos.

'Ambassadors, even when the weapons of war are lifted up, speak not otherwise than for the benefit of their State; and although they speak boldly according as it is their advantage, they are not to be put to death.'

Then I will declare what are the commands of the god Chandra. He bade me say, that in driving away, and destroying the rabbits who are appointed to guard the fountain which is consecrated to that deity, you have done ill; for, said he, they are my guards, and it is notorious that the figure of a rabbit is my emblem.*

The head elephant, upon hearing this being greatly alarmed, declared that they had offended through ignorance, and would never go to the fountain again. If this be your resolution, said the ambassador, go

* The Hindoo poets have imagined the moon as a deity sitting in a splendid chariot drawn by two antelopes, holding in his right hand a rabbit. This reminds the translator of what he must ever mention with extreme regret. He brought with him from India a large collection of Hindoo idols, amongst which was that of the moon above described. They were moulded under his own inspection from a set of paintings lent him for that purpose, and cast in metal, and of course cost him a great deal of money. They were exceedingly well packed, and arrived safe at the Custom-house, whence they were removed to one of the Company's warehouses, where they were exposed to public sale; but having been bought in by the proprietor's directions and carried to his house for the greater security in a coach, upon opening the box which contained them, to his inexpressible grief and mortification, he discovered that they had all been taken out of the cotton in which they had been packed, and treated so rudely that not a figure had escaped without the loss of some of its members.

this once, and make your submissions before the deity himself, whom you will see in the fountain, quite agitated with anger; and when you have pacified him, you may depart.—Accordingly, as soon as it was night, the ambassador Vijaya having conducted the chief of the elephants to the fountain, there showed him the image of the moon, trembling, as it were, upon the smooth surface of the water; and when he had made him bow down to it, in token of submission, he said,—Please your divinity! What hath been done having been done through ignorance, I pray thee pardon them! and upon saying this, he caused the elephant to depart. I repeat, therefore, "Great things may be effected," &c.

After that, continued the booby, I ventured to say, that our king too was powerful and valiant, upon which they laid hold of me with their beaks; and, asking me what business I had in their country, they carried me before their chief Chitra-varna; and when they had showed me to him, bowing to their king, they said,—Please your Highness, let this guilty booby be confined; for he dares, even whilst he is travelling in our land, to treat with contempt your royal feet! The king, in anger, demanded to know whence I came; and they informed him, that I was the servant of the goose Hiranya-garbha, and that I came from Karpura-dweepa.—After that, the minister, who was a vulture, asked me who was the prime minister in this country, and I told him, a Chakra-vaka,* whose name was Know-all.† You esteem him, replied the vulture, because he is your countryman; they say, indeed,

'A king should engage for his minister one who is a native of his own country; pure in all his ways, and cleanly in his dress; not one who is an outcast, addicted to idle pleasures, or too fond of women; but one of good repute, who is well versed in the rules of disputation, is of a firm mind, and expert in raising a revenue.'‡

A parrot next spoke, and observed, that as Karpura-dweepa was comprehended in Jambu-dweepa, the authority of his Majesty's feet certainly extended over that country also; to which the king of the birds replied,—Thus it is!

'Sovereigns, the libidinous, and children, with madmen, and such as are made vain by riches, are over-anxious for what is not attainable, and how much more so, for what is to be procured!'

Upon this, I said,—But that too large a government do not prosper, our sovereign has a territorial right, even over Jambu-dweepa.—Let it be declared

* A species of goose commonly called Brahmanee-goose. The Hindoos use no grease to their wheels.

† In the original Sarva-gna.

‡ Literally, *an upraiser of wealth.*

how, said the parrot, and where he will give proofs of it! And I replied,—In battle! At this their king laughing, said,—Go to thy master, and tell him to be well prepared; and upon that, I desired him to send his own ambassador also. Who shall go? said the king; for an embassy such a person is required as is described in these lines:

'An ambassador should be a trusty servant, endued with good qualifications, pure in his principles, clever, agreeable, unaddicted to fruitless pleasures, patient, and, with all, a Brahman* who is well acquainted with the moral and religious customs of strangers, and the nature of opposition.'

Although there are many such to be found, still a Brahman is to be preferred; for,

'He acteth according to the pleasure of his employer; he seeketh not wealth, and doth not withdraw himself from the presence of his lord, even in the hour of misfortune.'

This being the case, let the parrot go. Go, parrot, added the king, along with this person; and, upon thy arrival, make known our will. It shall be according to your Highness's commands, replied the parrot;

* This title has not hitherto been explained. As written in Sanskrit, it should be *Brahmana;* but, as before observed, the final short *a* is often dropped in repeating proper names in another language. It is a derivative from *Brahma*, the Supreme Being; *godly, divine, a divine.*

but this booby is a vile animal, and I am not used to go anywhere with a person of bad character. They say,

'A villain is sure to commit some evil action, and he succeedeth amongst good men. Seeta was seized by Ravana.* The ocean may have bonds.' †

It is not proper either to stay, or to go anywhere, along with an evil-disposed person. A goose suffered for staying with a crow, and a Varttaka ‡ for going with him.

How was this? demanded the king; and the parrot recounted the following story:

FABLE V.

ON a private road in Oojjayinee § there was a large Pippala tree, ‖ where lived together a goose and a crow. Once upon a time, in the cold season, a traveller came there, and having placed his bow and his arrows safe away under the tree, he went to sleep. A few minutes after, the shade of the tree passed away from his face, and presently it was covered by the scorching rays of the sun; upon seeing which, the

* Seeta was the wife of the god Ram, and Ravana the tyrant of Ceylon.

† The ocean is bound or confined by the dry land.

‡ Probably a sparrow.

§ The ancient city commonly called Ugein.

‖ The Indian poplar, commonly called Peepul.

goose, who was in the tree, expanded his wings, and again a shadow was formed as before. A little while after, in the enjoyment of a sound nap, the man happening to open his mouth, the crow muted into it, and flew out of the way. But the man waking, and seeing the goose upon the tree, concluded that it was he; so, being in a passion, he took his bow, and with an arrow drawn home to his ear, shot him dead upon the spot. I say, therefore, "It is not proper to stay," &c. I will now relate the history of the Varttaka, continued the parrot.

FABLE VI.

ONCE upon a time, all the birds of the air went in a body upon a pilgrimage to the seaside in honour of the eagle; and amongst the rest, the crow went accompanied by a Varttaka. As they flew along, the crow repeatedly stole and ate of some curds out of a pot which a farmer was carrying upon his head; but as soon as the man put the pot upon the ground, and saw the crow and the Varttaka together in the air, the former, being guilty, flew out of the way; but the latter, being but slow of flight, was caught and instantly killed. I say, therefore, "It is not proper either to stay, or to go," &c.

I then said,—Brother parrot, what is the reason thou railest thus against me? I esteem thee, nevertheless, as the feet of his Highness! Be it so, replied the parrot; but,

'When sincere and beloved friends are courted by those of bad character, it createth in me as much dread, as the sight of flowers out of season.'

Thy being a rascal is made evident to me from thy conversation; for if there should be any falling out between our two masters, thy tongue will be the cause.

Observe:

A fool will rejoice and be happy, even when offences are committed before his eyes. A certain wheelwright put his own wife with her gallant upon his head.

How was that? said the king; and the parrot related the following story:

FABLE VII.

IN Sree-nagara* there lived a wheelwright, whose name was Dull-wit;† who, though he believed his wife was false, had never, with his own eyes, seen her with her gallant. So he pretended that he was going out of town, but after he had gone a little way, he returned home, and privately hid himself under the sofa. In the meantime, the gallant, supposing

* Literally, *the fortunate city*. An ancient name of the city of Patna.

† In Sanskrit, Manda-mati.

the wheelwright was actually gone out of town, made his appearance; and, soon after, sat by the wife upon the sofa; where they began to converse without restraint. But just now, from the feel of something touching the under part of the sofa, she concluded that her husband was beneath, and so was a little disconcerted; upon which her friend said,—What is the reason thou dost not enjoy the present moment free from care? Thou appearest as if thou wert alarmed at something! Alas! replied the artful woman, he who is the lord of my life is gone abroad to-day; wherefore the city, though ever so full of inhabitants, to me appeareth a mere desert! Then is thy wheelwright, said the gallant, a subject worthy of all this tenderness? he who calls thee vile? Villain! exclaimed she, what is this thou sayest? Hear me!

'She is a virtuous woman, who, when spoken harshly to, and viewed with angry eyes, appeareth before her husband with a mild and placid countenance.

'The regions of eternal happiness are provided for those women, who love their husbands the same in a wilderness as in a city; be he a saint, or be he a sinner.

'A husband is a woman's first ornament, although himself be unadorned: but when she is without one, be she ornamented, she is not adorned.'

Thou art very fine, to be sure, and hast the appearance of a figure made up of garlands and flowers. Pray, do people ever worship thee?* My husband, if he chooses, can sell me to the gods, or give me to the Brahmans;† but what of that?

'I live in him living, and in him, my beloved, will I live when dead; for upon his death, to die after him is my firm resolve.'

For,

'The woman who followeth her husband‡ may remain in heaven for a million and a half of years, or for as many as there are hairs upon the body.

'As the snake-catcher by force draweth up the serpent from its hole; so, having taken her husband, she is to be raised into heaven.§

'Him should she attend whilst living, and him should she sleep with when dead, to whom her father

* As they are wont to do their idols, when adorned with garlands, and scented with sanders.

† By the laws of Manoo the Brahmans are allowed to marry three wives, one from each of the first three tribes. But this sentence cannot allude to that; it should rather seem to refer to the *nara-medha*, or human sacrifice, not uncommon in the earlier ages. It is not easy to conceive for what other purpose this good woman could be *sold to the gods*, or *given to the Brahmans*.

‡ The woman who voluntarily burneth herself upon the funeral pile with the dead corpse of her husband; which is very common, on the banks of the Ganges, at this day.

§ The meaning of this verse seems to be simply this, that the woman who followeth her husband in death will necessarily be raised into heaven.

may have given her, or her brother according to her father's will.' *

The foolish wheelwright, upon hearing all these fine speeches, said to himself,—O what a lucky fellow I am, to possess a wife who can speak of me with such tender love and affection! and, saying this, he rose with the sofa and its contents, and began to dance for joy. I repeat, therefore, "A fool," &c.

After this, continued the booby, as soon as the king had paid me the usual compliments, I was dismissed, and the parrot is coming behind. And now that I have apprised your Highness of all this, let that which is most proper be pursued. What! exclaimed the minister Chakra-vaka, the king's affairs have been forwarded, to the utmost of his abilities, by a booby, who happened to travel into a foreign country! But, please your Highness, he has acted according to his nature.

'One may give him a hundred instances from Holy Writ, that he should not dispute; still, it is the character of a fool to make a disturbance without a cause.'

Have done with these reproachful sayings! said the royal goose, and attend to what has been re-

* The laws of Manoo have given the father full authority over his daughters with respect to marriage.

ported. Please your Highness, replied the minister, I will speak to you in private; for,

'Those who are aware of it can interpret the mind from the changes of the eyes and other members: and even by the report of shape and complexion.'

And upon this, the rest withdrawing, the king and his minister were left by themselves. I think, said the minister, that this has been brought about by a spy sent by some officer of our government.* They say,

'A sick man is the best subject for a physician, and an active emissary for the officers of government; fools are the support of the learned, and a man of secrecy suits a king.'

Let the cause alone, said the king; at present it should be determined what ought to be done; then say. First, please your Highness, replied the minister, let a spy be sent, and then we shall learn the situation of the country, with its strength and weakness; for they say,

'A prince should have a spy to observe what is necessary, and what is unnecessary, to be done in his own, as well as in his enemy's country. He is the king's eye; and he who hath him not is blind.'

* Does he mean that some officer of their government had sent the booby, of his own authority, on purpose to pick a quarrel with the subjects of the peacock?

And let him take a second person with him, in whom he can confide; whom he shall send back, well disguised, charged with such secrets as are worthy to be communicated; whilst he himself remains upon the spot.

'He should command his emissaries to go disguised in company with those penitents, who travel with beards under pretence of studying in the courts of temples, and places of holy visitation.' *

The emissary we send should be one who will go about privately, and who will pass through land and water; and I know of no one, except the booby, who is endued with both these requisites; wherefore, let him be appointed. In the meantime, let all the inhabitants keep within our castle; and, till the messenger return, let profound secrecy be pursued; for,

'The deliberations of council are discovered if heard by six ears, as well as any private information; wherefore, a king should entrust his counsels only to himself and a second person.

'The injury which is done to princes, from their counsels being discovered, are not to be repaired, say those who are acquainted with the rules of policy.'

Well, said the king, now I have found such an

* Spies and private messengers, at this day, are generally disguised as pilgrims or mendicants, which characters are sacred in every part of India.

excellent emissary, what next? Your Highness, replied the minister, hath but to enter the field of battle, and victory will follow.

They were now interrupted by the entrance of one of the guards, who informed them, that there was a parrot waiting at the gate, just come from Jambudweepa. The king looked at the minister, and the minister said,—Lead him into a separate apartment, and some time hence he may be admitted. According to the commands of his Highness! said the guard; upon which he went away, taking the parrot with him.

So, said the king, Discord is arrived, and is in attendance! Yes, please your Highness, replied the minister; but discord is not necessity.*

'Is he a minister, or a counsellor, who, upon the first alarm, and without due consideration, adviseth his sovereign either to commence hostilities, or to quit his ground?

'A wise man may strive to conquer, but he should never fight; because victory, it is observed, cannot be constant to both the combatants.

'A man should never display his bravery who is unprepared for battle; nor bear the marks of defiance, until he hath experienced the abilities of his enemy.

* This expression is fully explained by the verse which follows it.

'Not more easily is a house* supported by mankind with a prop, than great achievements from trifling means. This is the great fruit of councils.'

But when we perceive that we are threatened with war, let preparations be made; for,

'The field is fruitful from having been cultivated in due season. It is the same with political measures; but these too advance slowly, not instantly, to maturity.

'When the quality of bravery is near, a great man's terrors are at a distance. In the hour of misfortune such a great man overcometh bravery.

'Great warmth, at first, is the certain ruin of every great achievement. Doth not water, although ever so cool, moisten the earth?'

Besides, an' please your Highness, king Chitra-varna is very strong; and,

'There is no ordinance obliging us to fight those who are stronger than ourselves. Such fighting, as it were, with an elephant, is the same as men's fighting against rocks.

'He is a fool who turneth upon his opponent, before he hath found a proper opportunity. The efforts of him, who contendeth with one stronger

* The original is *greeva*, the neck, which the translator has presumed a mistake for *greeha*, a house.

than himself, are as feeble as the exertions of an insect's wings.

'A prudent soldier, keeping within his tortoise-like shelter,* may, indeed, sustain the force of arms; and when occasion may suit, he may sally forth like an enraged serpent.'

Please your Highness, attend to this:

'One who is master of ever so little art may be able, on a great occasion, to root up trees with as much ease, as the current of a river the reeds and grass.'

Then let this ambassador, the parrot, be detained and amused, until we shall have put our fortifications in good condition.

'A single bowman standing upon the battlements fighteth a hundred; and a hundred, ten thousand: wherefore, a castle is to be preferred.

'What sovereign, whose country is furnished with strongholds, is subject to defeat? The prince of a country, without strongholds, is as a man who is an outcast of his tribe.

'He should build a castle with a large ditch and lofty battlements, and furnish it with machines for raising water; and its situation should be in a wood upon a hill, and where there are springs of fresh water.

* Figuratively, a castle or fortress.

'It should be spacious, but very uneven; and supplied with large store of liquor, grain, and money; and with gates and sally-ports; for these are the seven treasures of a castle.' *

Who, demanded the king, should be appointed to prepare our castle? The minister replied,

'Every one should be employed in that business he is best acquainted with. One who hath had no experience in civil affairs, although he may be a good soldier, would be at a loss in business of that kind.'

Then let the Sarasa † be called, concluded the minister. This being done accordingly, and the Sarasa arrived, the king gave him encouragement, and told him to put the castle in good order. The Sarasa, bowing, replied,—Please your Highness, the castle has lately been well examined. There is a large reservoir in it, in the centre there is an island, in which it is proper that there should be a store of grain laid up.

'A store of grain, O king! is the best of stores. A gem cast into the mouth will not support life.

'Of all sapid things, salt being esteemed the first,

* This and the preceding verse form a tolerable picture of a Hindoo fort.

† That beautiful tall bird of the stork species, commonly called a Syrus.

some should be laid in; for without it the beard is bedaubed.' *

Go then, said the king, and attend to what is necessary to be done. Just now a doorkeeper came in, and said,—Please your Highness, one Cloud-colour,† a crow, is just arrived from Singhala-dweepa,‡ who, with his attendants, desires to behold the foot of your Highness. A crow, said the king, is a wise bird, and a great observer of things; and that being the case, let him be received. He is so, replied the minister; but a crow is a land bird, and consequently of a different party to us; how then can he be received in contempt of our own party? It is said,

The fool who forsaketh his own party, and delighteth to dwell with the opposite side, may be killed by them; as was the case with the blue jackal.

How was this? demanded the king; and the minister related as follows:

FABLE VIII.

A CERTAIN jackal, as he was roaming about the borders of a town, just as his inclinations led him, fell

* This is probably some vulgar saying, which is not always founded upon truth.

† In the original, *megha-varna*.

‡ The island of Ceylon.

into a dyer's vat;* but being unable to get out, in the morning he feigned himself dead. At length, the master of the vat, which was filled with indigo, came, and seeing a jackal lying with his legs uppermost, his eyes closed, and his teeth bare, concluded that he was dead, and so, taking him out, he carried him a good way from the town, and there left him. The sly animal instantly got up, and ran into the woods; when, observing that his coat was turned blue, he meditated in this manner:—I am now of the finest colour! what great exaltation may I not bring about for myself? Saying this, he called a number of jackals together, and addressed them in the following words,—Know that I have lately been sprinkled † king of the forests, by the hands of the goddess herself who presides over these woods, with a water drawn from a variety of choice herbs. Observe my colour, and henceforward let every business be transacted according to my orders. The rest of the jackals, seeing him of such a fine complexion, prostrated themselves before him, and said,—According as your Highness commands! By this step he made himself honoured by his own relations, and so gained the supreme power over those of his own species, as well as all the other inhabitants of the forests. But

* A dyer's vat, in Hindostan, is a large pan sunk in the ground, often in the little court before the dyer's house.

† The Hindoos use holy water instead of oil.

after a while, finding himself surrounded by a levée of the first quality, such as the tiger and the like, he began to look down upon his relations; and, at length, he kept them at a distance. A certain old jackal perceiving that his brethren were very much cast down at this behaviour, cried,—Do not despair! If it continue thus, this imprudent friend of ours will force us to be revenged. Let me alone to contrive his dowfall. The lion, and the rest who pay him court, are taken by his outward appearance; and they obey him as their king, because they are not aware that he is nothing but a jackal: do something then by which he may be found out. Let this plan be pursued: Assemble all of you in a body about the close of the evening,* and set up one general howl in his hearing; and I'll warrant you, the natural disposition of his species will incline him to join in the cry; for,

'Whatever may be the natural propensity of any one, is very hard to be overcome. If a dog were made king, would he not gnaw his shoe straps?'

And thus, the tiger discovering that he is nothing but a jackal, will presently put him to death. In short, concluded the minister, the plan was executed,

* The jackals seldom make their appearance till after sunset, when they sally forth in large troops, and "font retentir l'air de leurs aboyemens," as the compiler of "Description Historique et Geographique de l'Inde," expresses it. Tome i. p. 37.

and the event was just as it had been foretold. They say,

'An intimate enemy is acquainted with everything which relateth to one: our blemishes, our hearts, and our degree of courage.'

I repeat, therefore, "The fool," &c.

Although it be thus, replied the king, still as he is come a great way, let him appear; for such is the resolution of inquiries made respecting whom we ought to entertain.—Please your Highness, said the minister, the spy is despatched, and the castle is put in complete order, wherefore the parrot should receive assurances of our pacific disposition, and be permitted to depart. But,

'As it is possible that the revolutions of council may be defeated by the designs of a sharp ambassador, a sovereign should always regard him as a spy.'

After this a council was formed, and both the parrot and the crow were desired to attend. The parrot, with a slight inclination of his head, seated himself upon a stool which was presented to him, and then delivered his commission in the following words: —Sir, the most illustrious Maha-rajah* Chitra-varna commandeth thee, Hiranya-garbha, if thou hast any

* Literally, *great Rajah.* A title in these days by no means confined to men of royal or even noble extraction.

occasion for life or fortune, instantly to repair into his presence, and prostrate thyself at his feet; or else, to think of retiring to live in some other country! The king, in anger, exclaimed,—Ha! have we no one about us? The crow, Cloud-colour, instantly rose up and cried out,—Give but the word, and I will kill this infamous parrot! In the meantime, the minister, who was engaged in pacifying the king, repeated these lines:

'That is not a council, wherein there are no sages; they are not sages, who do not declare men's duty; that is not a duty, in which there is not virtue; and that is not virtue from which fear approacheth us.'

The law speaks thus: but, moreover, this parrot is a Brahman; and they say also,

'An ambassador, although he be a barbarian, is not to be put to death; for he is only the mouth of his master: no, not even when the weapons of war are lifted up; and how much less, if he be a Brahman!

'An ambassador never payeth any regard either to his own inferiority, or others' superiority; but under the decree of fate, that he is not punishable, he speaketh without reserve.'

Upon hearing these maxims, both the king and the crow were pacified; and the parrot got up and went away. But upon a motion of the minister's, things having been explained to him, he was brought back, and dismissed with presents of golden ornaments, rich dresses, and the like.

The parrot returned to the Vindhya mountains, where paying his respects to Chitra-varna his own sovereign, the king no sooner perceived him, than he called out,—Well, parrot, what intelligence hast thou brought me? What sort of a country is it? Please your Highness, replied the parrot, the sum of my intelligence is this,—Let preparations be made for war! As to the country, it is a portion of the heavenly regions; then how is it possible to describe it? The peacock king, upon hearing this, sent for his chiefs, and sat down to consult with them. On the subject of the war, said the king, which is presently to be entered into, advise what is proper to be done; for, again I say, war is absolutely resolved upon. They say,

'Brahmans are ruined when discontented, like sovereigns when contented. Modesty is ruin to a harlot, and immodesty to women of good repute.'

Amongst the rest, there was a vulture whose name was Far-see,* who arose and said,—Please your Highness, Fate would not be idle in fighting with thee; for,

'When sons, with friends and attendants, are firmly

* In the original, *doora-darsee*.

attached, and in opposition to the enemy, then war may be commenced.'

Let my minister observe what I am about to order, said the king; let the services of these my officers be engaged by an advance of a part of their pay; and then let the soothsayer * be called, and let him fix upon a lucky moment † for us to begin our march. Yet, please your Highness, observed the minister, it is not proper to march rashly; for they say,

'Those fools who rashly, and without investigation, rush upon the forces of the enemy, will doubtlessly be embraced with the edges of their swords.'

Minister, replied the king, thou shouldst not endeavour to break the force of my ardour. Tell me rather how one who wishes for conquest advanceth into the country of the enemy. Please your Highness, said the minister, this subject too if pursued may yield fruit; for they say,

'What is the use of advice given to a sovereign according to the authority of books, if it be not followed? A patient will never recover his health merely from the description of a medicine.'

* The Hindoos of the present age do not undertake any affair of consequence without consulting their astrologers, who are always Brahmans.

† The lucky and unlucky days are generally pointed out in their almanacs, but as these are always written in Sanskrit, none but the Brahmans can explain them.

But as the commands of majesty are not to be neglected, I will proceed to repeat what I have heard upon the subject of war. Please to attend, your Highness:

'Troops, with everything which can make them formidable, should be stationed upon the rivers, upon the mountains, in the woods, in the strongholds, and wherever else there is danger.

'The Adhyaksha* should march before, accompanied by the bravest men; in the centre the seraglio,† the swamee,‡ the treasure chest, the magazines of provisions, and everything else which may be valuable.

'On each flank the horse, on the two flanks of the horse the chariots,§ on the two flanks of the chariots the elephants, and on the two flanks of the elephants the foot.‖

'In the rear should march the Sena-pati¶ occasionally encouraging such as seem to be melancholy.

* Literally, *overseer.* Probably an officer like our quartermaster-general.

† The original word is *kalatram*, which signifies either *wives* or a *place of safety.*

‡ This word in the common acceptation means *master;* but in this place, probably, either the prince, or his commander-in-chief.

§ Although these are disused in battle at present, they are constantly mentioned in their ancient books, as a necessary part of an army.

‖ The horse, chariots, elephants, and foot, are, in Sanskrit, called *the four members of an army.*

¶ Literally, *army-master;* a general.

And the king should take the field accompanied by his counsellors and choicest heroes.

'The uneven ground, swampy places, and hills, should be cleared by the elephants; the plains by the horse, the rivers by boats, and the foot should be employed everywhere.

'Upon the arrival of the rains it is best to march with elephants only, they say; but at other times, with all the four distinction of troops.

'Amongst hills, and in narrow passes, it is proper that the chief should be guarded by some of his best troops; and the same when he is asleep, with watchful care.

'The army should strive to destroy, and distress the enemy by rolling stones down from the tops of steep places; * and as soon as they enter the enemy's country, the Attavika † should be formed before.

'Wherever the chief is, there should the treasure chest be; for without treasure there is no superiority. And some of it should be distributed amongst the principal officers; for who will not fight for one who giveth freely?

'Man is not a servant for the man, but for the thing. A chief's consequence, or insignificance, dependeth upon his having wealth, or no wealth.

* It is common to see stones, formed round for this purpose, placed upon the parapets of Hindoo fortresses, at this day.

† These seem to have been *hatchet-men* or *pioneers*.

'The troops should fight without breaking; and they should defend one another. Whatever military stores there may be should be put in the centre of the ranks.

'And when the chief hath given check to the enemy, he should endeavour to distress the country. Upon level ground he should fight with chariots and his horse; and in places overflowed with water, either with boats or elephants.

'Amongst trees and bushes he should fight with bows and arrows; and upon open ground, with sword and shield. And he should always endeavour to destroy, or render useless, the enemy's straw, corn, water, and firewood.

'He should destroy likewise their reservoirs, their ramparts, and their ditches and trenches. The chief's elephants should be the first in the army, and not disordered.

'They say, he who fighteth with elephants and camels, fighteth, as it were, with his own arms. The horse is the strength of the army. The horse is as a moving bulwark.

'Wherefore, the chief who hath most horse in a land fight is victorious. Those who fight mounted on horses are hard to be defeated, even by the hosts of heaven; for let the enemy be at ever so great a distance, they are, as it were, in their hands.

'The chief employment for the foot is fighting,

guarding the whole army, and clearing the roads about.

'The best kind of troops are declared to be those who are naturally brave, skilled in the exercise of arms, attached, inured to fatigue, renowned, and soldier-like.

'Men, O prince, do not fight so well in this world, even for very large pecuniary rewards, as for honours bestowed by their commander.

'A small army consisting of chosen troops is far better than a vast body chiefly composed of rabble; for when the bad give way, the good are inevitably broken in consequence.

'He who wisheth for victory should endeavour to harass the enemy without distressing his own troops. An enemy's army which has been harassed for a long time, may be easily defeated.

'There is not a better counsellor than a competitor, for the overthrow of an enemy; wherefore great pains should be taken to raise such a claimant.

'Having entered into a confederacy with some one amongst the chief's sons, or with one of his principal counsellors, at length, it will be proper, with a firm resolution, to provoke him to fight.

'And when a chief shall have given him an overthrow by means of his nearest friends, he may put his enemy to death.' *

* This verse is defective in the original.

What is the use of saying so much upon the subject? said the king, interrupting him:

'One's own exaltation is another's tribulation, and both, they say, is policy. Having granted this, our fine language is contradicted by our actions.'*

The minister, smiling at this, replied,—It is entirely so; but,

'One is lofty, powerful, and a villain; whilst another is guided and restrained by moral laws. When shall we find the same superiority in light and darkness?'†

At length the king got up and resolved to march at the time appointed by his astrologer; but just now the Purohita‡ met him, accompanied by a spy, and told him, that king Chitra-varna was almost arrived, and that at present he was near the Malaya mountains; that the construction of a castle was instantly to be resolved, for the vulture was a very wise minister; and that from the tenor of his conversation there was reason to believe, that he had a spy even then within the castle. To all this the minister replied, that if there was a spy, it could be no one but the crow, whom they had entertained.

* Morality forbids us to advance our fortunes at the expense of others; but policy pays no attention to this injunction.

† Good and evil.

‡ Spiritual guide.

That can never be, replied the king; for if he had been so, how came it to pass that he showed such readiness to punish the parrot? And besides, war was not resolved till very lately upon the return of their ambassador the parrot. Nevertheless, answered the minister, it is proper to suspect one who came to us as he did. True, replied the king, provided he be guilty of any improper action; but,

'A stranger, if well-disposed, is a friend; but a friend, if ill-disposed towards one, is a stranger. A distemper, although generated in the body, is malignant; whilst a drug produced in the woods proveth salutary.'

King Subhraka had a servant, by name Veera-vara, who in a very short time offered up his own son.

How was that? said the minister; and the king related the following tale:

FABLE IX.

IN former days I used to amuse myself with a certain female of my own species, whose name was Karpoora-manjaree,* and who was the daughter of the royal gander Karpoora-keli, in a pleasure lake belonging to king Subhraka. One day a young man, whose name was Veera-vara, and who proved to be a Rajah-

* White pearl.

putra* come from some distant country, presented himself before the porter who stood at the king's gate, and addressed him in the following words:—I am a soldier in search of employment; pray procure me a sight of the king. The porter went to his master, and, bowing, told him that there was a soldier at the gate, just arrived from some distant country, who said his name was Veera-vara; and the king commanded him to be introduced. Accordingly, the porter conducted the stranger into the presence of his master; to whom, respectfully bowing, he addressed himself as follows:—Sir, if thou hast any occasion for my service, let my pay be fixed. The king asked him, how much? and he replied, four hundred suvarnas † a day. What weapons hast thou? demanded the king. My two arms, replied the soldier, and my sword, which makes a third. This will not do, concluded the king; upon which the soldier bowed, and took his leave. The minister happening to be present, said,—Please your Highness, give him four days' pay, and learn what sort of a man he is, and what assistance he can be of. According to the minister's advice, the man being called back, they gave him Tamboola,‡ and four days' pay in advance;

* Literally, *the son of a Rajah.* A warlike tribe, commonly called Rajpoots.

† Gold coins.

‡ The betel leaf; but, in this place, the whole composition commonly called *pawn* by the natives of Bengal, and *betel* by the Euro-

to the expenditure of which the king very privately attended, and found that he gave one moiety to the gods and the Brahmans, one-fourth to the poor, and spent the remainder in food and amusements; and that after performing these several praiseworthy actions, he attended sword in hand at the king's gate day and night, and never went to his lodgings without his master's express permission.

On the fourteenth night of what is called the dark side of the moon, the king heard a noise like one bitterly crying, upon which he called out to know who was waiting at the door, and his faithful Veera-vara answering that he was there, he ordered him to pursue the crying which they heard; so, saying, I obey your Highness's commands, away he ran. In the meantime, the king reflected in this manner:—I have done wrong to send this soldier away by himself in such a dark cloudy night. I will even go too and see what is the matter. So saying, he took his sword, and thus followed till he got without the city; and presently after he saw the soldier with a female endued with perfect youth and beauty, and richly attired, who was weeping. Who art thou, and why dost thou weep? demanded Veera-vara. I am, said the female, the goddess Sree,* the fortune of king

peans, must be understood; which, every one knows, is given in India by a superior as an inviolable token of friendship, favour, and protection.

* The goddess of good fortune.

Subhraka's dominions, who hath long dwelt happily under the shadow of his wings; but, alas! I am now about to flee to some other place of refuge. What, O goddess, said the soldier, will induce thee to tarry still longer here? If, replied the goddess, thou wilt offer up thy own son Sakti-vara, who is distinguished by two-and-thirty marks,* to the goddess who presideth over the welfare of all nature,† then will I remain here for a much longer period of time; and saying this, she vanished from his sight.

Veera-vara now went home, and called up his son and his wife, who were both asleep; who having risen accordingly, he related to them everything which had passed with the goddess. His son, the moment he had concluded, exclaimed in a transport of joy,—O how fortunate I am, who can thus be the means of preserving my sovereign and his dominions! Then, O father, what occasion is there for any further hesitation or delay; since the assistance of this body is at all times ready upon such an occasion as this? For they say,

'A good man should forsake wealth, and even life itself, for another. It is good to sacrifice one's self

* What these are the translator is unable to explain.

† This long epithet is expressed, in the original, in two words, *sarva mangala*, which is one of the titles of Bhavanee, the consort of Seeva. In her destructive quality she is called Kalee (a name derived from Kala, time), and it was to her, under this image, that human sacrifices were wont to be offered, to avert any threatened evil.

for a holy person upon the approach of his destruction.'

This simple saying belongs particularly to our tribe;* then if I am not permitted to do so, by what other act will the preservation of the prosperity of this great country be secured? Having considered this proposal, they all went to the temple of the goddess; and when they had worshipped her image, the father Veera-vara addressed her in these words:—O goddess! let Subhraka our sovereign be prosperous! and let this victim be accepted! Saying which, he cut off his son's head. Thus, said he to himself, have I earned the wages which I received from my sovereign; and now let me pay the forfeit of my son's life! and instantly he cut off his own head. His wife too, overpowered with grief for her husband and son, followed their example. The king, filled with astonishment at the scene before him, said to himself:

'Such little animals as myself come into life, and die away without end; but there never has been, nor ever will be, in this world one like unto him!'

Oh, I can have no further enjoyment of these my dominions! Saying this, he lifted up his sword to cut off his head also; but on the instant, she on whom dependeth the happiness of all, making herself

* To the tribe of Rajah-putra, or soldiers.

evident under human form, seized him by the hand, and said,—My son, forbear this rashness! At present thy kingdom is not subdued!* The king prostrated himself before her, and said,—O goddess! of what use to me is dominion, or even life? If thou hast any compassion for me, O let Veera-vara, with his family, be restored to life; or if it be not thy will, permit me to pursue the path wherein I was found by thee! The goddess replied,—I am well pleased with this thy noble generosity and tenderness; then go thy ways, and prosper; and let this man, his wife, and son, all rise up and live! The king rendered thanks, and returned unobserved to an apartment of his palace to sleep. Veera-vara too being restored to life, together with his wife and son, he conducted them home.

Veera-vara being again on guard at the king's door, and being questioned by him respecting the person who was heard crying, replied, that upon her being seen she became invisible, and that there were no further tidings of her.† The king was exceedingly well pleased at this, and said within himself,—What a praiseworthy man he was, repeating these lines:

'He should speak kindly, without meanness; he

* The goddess Sree hath not yet forsaken thy dominions.

† From the tenor of this period, it should seem, that the king, when he followed Veera-vara, did not go near enough to observe all that passed with the goddess Sree.

should be valiant, without boasting; he should be generous, shedding his bounty into the dish of the worthy; he should be resolute, but not harsh.'

This is the character of a great man! In this there is all!

In the morning early the king assembled a special council; and when he had publicly proclaimed the proceedings of the night, he bestowed the government of Karnatta* upon his generous deliverer. After this, concluded the royal goose, must every one who cometh unasked be a villain? The truth is, there are three sorts amongst such too: good, bad and indifferent.

The minister replied,

'Is he a minister who, in obedience to his sovereign's pleasure, payeth attention to what should not be done, as if it were proper to be done? It is better that the heart of the master should suffer pain, than that he should be ruined by doing that which ought not to be done.'

Hear this, please your Highness:

The good which hath been gained by one will also be gained by me. But the barber who wished for wealth, having through his infatuation killed a beggar, is put to death himself.

* The country we call Carnatic.

How came that about? said the king; and the minister related the following story:

FABLE X.

In the country of Ayodhya * there was a man, by name Choora-mani,† who, being exceedingly anxious for the acquisition of wealth, offered up his prayers with great fervour, to him in whose diadem is a crescent; ‡ and at length, one night, when he had been purified of his sins, that deity appeared to him in his sleep, and addressed him in these words:—In the morning early, having shaved thyself, stand out of sight with a stick in thy hand; and when thou shalt see a beggar coming into the yard, thou wilt beat him with thy stick without mercy; for the said beggar will have with him a pot of gold, which may serve to make thee as happy as thou canst wish for the rest of thy life. The instructions of the god were followed, and success attended; but the whole transaction having been observed by the barber, who came to shave the man, said to himself,—Ho, ho! this is the way to get money, is it? Why then may not I do the same? From that moment the barber used every day to conceal himself with a large stick in his hand, waiting for the coming of a beggar; and

* The province of Oude.

† Crown-jewel.

‡ One of the titles of Seeva.

at length, when one came, he beat him so unmercifully, that he died; and the consequence was, that the barber was put to death by the officers of justice for the crime. I say, therefore, "The good," &c.

The king replied,

'How is a stranger to be found out by the repetition of a parcel of old stories, whether he be one who hath no motive, or a friend, or one who would betray one's confidence?'

Let the crow alone, and let us pursue what we have to do. Chitra-varna is now in the neighbourhood of Malaya. What is to be done? The minister replied,—'Tis true he is come; but I have heard from the mouth of a trusty spy, that Chitra-varna hath treated the wise counsels of that great minister the vulture with contempt; and therefore the fool may be defeated; for they say,

'The enemy who is either avaricious, subject to passion, unruly, treacherous, violent, fearful, unsteady, or a fool, is easily to be defeated, we are told.'

Then, before he shall have given orders to invest our castle, let the Sarasa and other generals be sent out upon the rivers, into the woods, upon the mountains, and through the passes, to destroy his forces. They say,

'If an enemy's army be fatigued by a long march,

confined by rivers, hills, or forests; terrified by the apprehension of dreadful fires,* distressed by hunger, thirst, and the like;

'With their best provisions spoilt, afflicted with pestilence and famine, not steady, not numerous, embarrassed by rains and winds;

'Incommoded by dirt, dust, or water, or destitute of good quarters; a prince may defeat it, and under any circumstances like these.

'Or if an enemy be found sleeping in the day, from the great fatigue of watching for fear of a surprise, thus overpowered for want of rest, one may at all times easily defeat him.'

Wherefore, let these generals march against the forces of that impetuous peacock, and fight them, either by day or night, as they may find it most expedient.

This advice being executed accordingly, the army of Chitra-varna was overthrown, and a great many of its principal leaders fell in the battle. Chitra-varna was exceedingly cast down at this event, and said to his minister the vulture,—Has this happened through neglect; or have I been wanting in conduct?

'Never before now was empire gained, thus to be

* The armies of the native princes of India, who are seldom provided with tents, often screen themselves from the inclemencies of the weather with temporary coverings of reeds or rushes, and their cantonments are generally made of mats and straw.

lost! The want of prudence destroyeth fortune, even as sickness the greatest beauty.

'One who is expert gaineth fortune; he who eateth but what is wholesome, health; and the healthy, ease; the diligent, the end of knowledge; and he who is well disciplined, virtue, profit, and reputation.'

The vulture replied,—Please your Highness,

'A king, although he be not himself experienced, may, if he has one old in wisdom about him, deprive another of his good fortune; like a tree which groweth by the water's side.

'Drinking, women, hunting, gaming, fondness for dress, harshness of speech, and severity, are great blemishes in a prince.

'Riches and prosperity are not possible to be acquired by such as pursue power with sudden violence, nor by those whose minds are at a loss for the means; for fortune dwelleth in good conduct and noble resolution.

'Betel * is pungent, bitter, spicy,† and sweet; it is alkaline and astringent; it expelleth wind, destroyeth phlegm, killeth worms, and subdueth bad smells; it beautifieth the mouth,‡ removeth impurities, and

* In the Sanskrit, Tambula. The composition of what Europeans call betel is too generally known to require a note.

† This word was substituted by the translator in the room of one which seemed to him an error in the original.

‡ Stains it red.

kindleth the fire of love. Betel, my friend, possesseth these thirteen qualities, hardly to be found, even in the regions of heaven.' *

But, continued the vulture, your Highness, trusting to your own strength and courage, and from mere rashness, paid no attention to the counsels I laid before you, and treated me with harshness of speech.

'Upon what minister do not the errors of conduct fall? What sore arm is not fretted by a garment of hair? † Whom doth not fortune make proud? Whom doth not death destroy? To whom do not the things which women do, give cause of great uneasiness?

'A brave man destroyeth his enemies, be they ever so great; even as prudence overcometh misfortune, an enlightened understanding grief, the sun darkness, and sorrow happiness.'

But, at that time, I said within myself,—This my master is certainly destitute of wisdom, or else he would be guided by my counsels; for they say,

'What will the wise precepts of books do for him

* The translator is of opinion this accurate description of the qualities and properties of betel has no business in this place. [Betel stands metaphorically for good counsel.—H. M.]

† When are not the poor oppressed? or, doth not one misfortune bring on another?

who is destitute of natural wisdom? What will a mirror do for him who hath no eyes?'

And, for these reasons, I remained silent.—The king, upon hearing this, joining his hands, said,—I agree that the fault was all my own. But, in our present distress, thou shouldst instruct me how I shall be able to retreat, with the few troops I have left, to the Vindhya mountains. The minister now resolved, within his own mind, that he ought to be reconciled to his master, recollecting this saying:

'Anger should always be restrained in the presence of the gods, before one's master, sovereign, or a Brahman; in a cowhouse;* and not less where there are children, and aged or sick people.'

Do not be alarmed! said he to the king, smiling as he spoke; be comforted! They say,

'The wisdom of ministers shineth most upon the breach of concord, and when affairs are fallen into confusion. In peace, who is not wise?

'If fools undertake ever so little, they willingly become independent; whilst those who perform great actions, and are men of wisdom and experience, remain attached.'

This being the case, when by thy valour thou shalt

* Probably from the danger of being tossed, rather than out of respect to those holy animals.

have penetrated the castle of the enemy, I will, without delay, conduct thee, together with honour, glory, and thy army, safe back to the Vindhya mountains. How shall this be accomplished, said the peacock king, with so small a force? Please your Highness, replied the vulture, the whole shall come to pass. But as the opposite of dilatoriness is a quality absolutely necessary for a conqueror to ensure success, let instant orders be given for the blockade of the enemy's castle.

Soon after this resolution, a spy came to the royal goose Hiranya-garbha, and told him that the peacock king, by the advice of the vulture his minister, small as his army was, had resolved to march and block up the castle gates. What is to be done now? said the king. Let our army, replied the minister, be divided into good and bad, and let presents be made to the whole, according to their deserts, of money, cloth, and the like; for it is said,

'Fortune never forsaketh the prince who standeth with an open hand in the squares and public places. A trifle, thus acquired, is esteemed far above a thousand pieces of gold found by chance in the road.

'A prince should be at an extraordinary expense on eight occasions: at a sacrifice, at a wedding, in times of distress, after the overthrow of an enemy, in any meritorious work, in entertaining friends, upon women who are dear to him, and in relieving relations who are in want.

'A fool, from the dread of ever so trifling expense, ruineth everything he undertaketh. What wise man would, from extreme scrupulousness, entirely forsake a clean pot?'*

How, demanded the king; is it proper to be extravagant on any occasion, when they say,—"A man should keep his riches against accidents," &c.? How can one who is fortunate, said the minister, meet with accidents? Because fortune sometimes leaves one, replied the king. Hoarded treasure, observed the minister, is often lost; then away with parsimony, and let thy brave soldiers be distinguished by gifts and honours.

'Those who have been preferred, and are well contented; such as are regardless of life, and have been proved; with those of noble birth, who have been treated with marks of distinction; will, all of them, be victorious over the forces of the enemy.

'A trifling force, consisting of only five hundred heroes, who are good soldiers, well experienced in the art of war, and resolute, when formed into a compact body, will beat a whole army of their enemies.

'The greatest qualities for a prince are, veracity,

* Hindoos generally boil their food in earthen pots, which they never use a second time.

courage, and generosity. If a sovereign be destitute of these, he will certainly acquire the state of being talked of with contempt.'

Ministers, likewise, should be distinguished and promoted; for,

'He should be employed in affairs of life and fortune, with whom is our protection, and with whom is confided our income and expense.' *

For,

'The prince who hath for his advisers, knaves, women, children, or fools, neglecteth the purification of imprudence, and is overwhelmed in the hour of necessity.'

Observe, your Highness, that

'The earth is bountiful unto him who hath neither extreme joy nor anger in his breast, who hath a treasure with but little expense, and who hath servants who are always vigilant.

'A prince who is well furnished with treasures, and other means, should never neglect or despise his ministers.'

For,

'When a king, blinded by his rashness, is about to

* This verse, in the original, is so full of errors and consequent obscurity, that nothing but the context could have discovered the meaning.

be overwhelmed in the ocean of his affairs, a friendly minister stretcheth out his hand from the dry land to assist him.'

Just now the crow Cloud-colour came in, and, bowing, cried,—Please your Highness, look yonder! The enemy is at the gate anxious for battle. But issue your commands, and I will sally forth and display my prowess, by which action I shall pay the debt I owe your Highness! Not so, not so! replied Know-all; it is by no means proper to go forth to fight; if it were, there would have been no occasion for our taking shelter in the castle.

'The alligator, matchless as he is, when he quitteth the water, is without power. Were even the lion to forsake the forests, he would doubtless be upon a level with the jackal.'

Please your Highness, said the crow, go yourself, and see the battle.

'A king having advanced his forces, should fight, overlooking them; for who will not truly act the lion when his master standeth over him?'

After this, they all marched to the castle gate, and fought a great battle. In the meantime Chitra-varna, the peacock king, addressed his minister to fulfil his promise immediately, who replied,—Attend, please your Highness:

'A fortification is declared to be weak, when it is unable to hold out a long time, is extremely small, and very much exposed; or when commanded by a weak and unfortunate officer.'

But seeing that is not the case here,

'There are four ways to take a fort, which are these: creating divisions, long blockading, surprise, and storming.'

At present, only let the battle be maintained to the utmost of our power, concluded the vulture.

Early in the morning, even before the sun was up, when the battle had commenced at all the four gates of the castle, the crow, who was in the inside, contrived to set fire to every house. There was now a confused rumour that the enemy had got possession; hearing which, and, at the same time, seeing a vast number of houses in flames, the troops of the royal goose, with all the private inhabitants, fled to the waters for security; according to this saying:

'Whatever hath been well consulted and well resolved, whether it be to fight well, or to run away well, should be carried into execution in due season, without any further examination.'

The king having been thus abandoned by all but the Sarasa, and being by nature a slow walker, was made prisoner by the cock, who was the peacock's general; upon which he addressed the Sarasa in these words:—General Sarasa, when I shall be no more, thou must not destroy thyself; but as thou hast it still in thy power to make thy escape, then go upon the waters, and, with the will of the Omniscient, place Choora-karna my son upon the throne. O my royal master, replied the Sarasa, do not talk thus, for it is more than I can bear. May the king still triumph over his enemies as long as the sun and moon shall last! I will again assume the command of the castle, and then let the foe enter besmeared with my blood!

'A master is hard to be found, who is patient, generous, and a judge of merit; or a servant, who is honest, clever, and attached.'

Attend to this, please your Highness: If after having quitted the field of battle there were no fear of death, it would be proper to go hence; but is not death inevitable to all things? Besides, it would tarnish my reputation to quit thee now.

'In this world, raised up for our purification, and to prevent our wandering in the regions below,* the resolution to sacrifice one's own life to the safety of another is attained by the practice of virtue.'

* The original word is *veechee*, which only means a particular division of those regions.

Besides, thou art the sovereign and master, who is always to be guarded and protected.

'When Prakriti is forsaken by her lord, great as she is, she doth not survive it.* When life hath taken its departure, though Dhanwantari † be the physician, what can he do?

'In the sovereign the whole world openeth and shutteth its eyes. Thus the lotus of the waters, upon the rising of the sun, reviveth upon his revival.

'The sovereign, the minister, territory, strongholds, treasure, forces, and friends, are the members of government; also the nobles, and the order of citizens.'

But, of all these, the sovereign is the principal member. Here the cock flew upon the royal goose, and began to wound him with his bill and claws; but the Sarasa screened his master under his own body; and although he himself was torn almost to pieces by the cock's beak and spurs, he still covered him till he got him safe into the water. Immediately after, the Sarasa pecked the cock to death; but at last, being attacked by a large party of birds, he lost his own life. Chitra-varna, the peacock king, now enters the

* To understand how this verse is applicable to the subject, it is necessary the reader be informed, that by the word Prakriti (here signifying *that from which all things are made: Principle,—Nature* personified as a beautiful female—the Hindoo *Eve*), is meant *the principal men, the nobility.*

† The Æsculapius of the Hindoos.

castle, and having plundered it of everything that had been left in it, he marched out again, saluted by his followers with shouts of victory!

The young princes now said to the Vishnu-Sarma, In our opinions, the Sarasa, in having thus preserved his master, at the expense of his own life, was the most virtuous bird in the army.

'Cows bring forth young, all of the same shape as their parents; but few produce a king of the herd whose horns stroke his shoulders.' *

May the exalted being, replied Vishnu-Sarma, who, of his own accord, purchaseth the regions of happiness with his own body, enjoy them, and be attended by Vidhya-dharees. They say,

'Such brave men as shed their blood in battle in their sovereign's cause, and such men as are faithful and grateful to their masters, are those who go to heaven.†

'Whenever a hero is killed, surrounded by the enemy, he obtaineth for himself those regions which are without decay; provided he doth not show cowardice.'

You have now, sirs, heard everything which relates to Disputing, concluded Vishnu-Sarma. We

* Having long horns.

† For a time measured by their virtues.

have, replied the young princes, and are exceedingly well pleased. May that which follows, said Vishnu-Sarma, produce the same effect.

'May no possessor of the earth ever have occasion to dispute with elephants, horses, and foot soldiers! May his enemies, defeated by the cleansing counsels of policy, take shelter in the caverns of the mountains!'

CHAPTER IV.

OF MAKING PEACE.

NOW, said the young princes, please to inform us of what relates to Making Peace. Attend then, replied Vishnu-Sarma; this is the introduction to it:

At the conclusion of a great battle, in which the troops of both kings have suffered, a treaty is presently brought about by the two ministers, the Vulture and the Chakravaka.

How was this? demanded the young princes; and Vishnu-Sarma related as follows:

FABLE I.

THE royal goose, after his escape, asked who it was that set fire to the castle; whether one of the enemy or some of their own party? and his minister, Chakravaka, replied,—Please your Highness, that unnecessary connection of yours, the crow Cloud-colour, together with his attendants, is no longer to be seen; wherefore, I conclude that it was contrived by him. The king, after a few moments' consideration exclaimed,—It is even so! It is my own evil seeking!

'The fault shall be for ever his, and no more the minister's, by whom I believe our affairs, so well designed for our own advantage, were ruined.'

They say, replied the minister,

'The man who meeting with the rugged paths of life, doth not know that they are evils of his own seeking,* is no philosopher.

He who doth not pay due regard to the advice of such friends as have his welfare at heart, may suffer for it; like the foolish tortoise, who fell from a piece of wood and was killed.

How was this? demanded the king; and his minister related the following story:

FABLE II.

IN Magadha-desa † there is a large piece of water which is distinguished by the appellation Phullotpala,‡ where lived together for a long time two geese; and they had a tortoise for their friend, who dwelt with them. Some fishermen coming that way, said to themselves,—To-morrow early we must con-

* By the vices of a former life.

† The ancient name of the country about Gya.

‡ Relating to the production of aquatic flowers.

trive to catch some turtle, and other fish. This having been overheard by the tortoise, he said,—My friends, you have heard the conversation of these fishermen, then what do you think I had best do? The two geese replied,—We shall know by-and-by what is fit to be done. Not so! what is conceived proper, that should be done immediately.

These two, Fate-not-come, and Wit-against-it-when-come, both of them happily flourish; whilst What-will-be loseth his life.

How was that? demanded the two geese; and the tortoise related the following story:

FABLE III.

FORMERLY, in this very piece of water, when the same danger threatened them as now threatens us, it was foreseen by three fish. One of them, whose name was Fate-not-come,* said,—I will sink deep in the water for security; and, saying so, down he went. The second, who was called Wit-against-it-when-come,† said,—In an affair which is about to come to pass, one should not proceed without an authority; now it is said,

* In the original, *anagata-vidhata.* It was necessary to translate the names, to save the spirit of the fable.

† In Sanskrit, *pratyutpanna-mati.*

He is a wise man who can conquer an accident when it happeneth. A merchant's wife charged her gallant with theft, before her husband's face.

The third fish, who was called What-will-be,* asked him how that was; and the second fish related as follows:

FABLE IV.

AT Vikrama-pura † there lived a merchant, whose name was Samudra-doota,‡ and his wife, who was called Ratna-prabha,§ was always amusing herself with one or other of the servants; according to these sayings:

They do not carry their observations so far as to examine limbs and features; for, whether handsome or ugly, it is all the same to them, provided he be a man.'

Again,

'Unto women no man is found disagreeable,' &c.

In another place they say,

'A sacred law which hath been ever so well considered, is still to be reconsidered; a king who hath been satisfied is still to be apprehended; a young

* In the original, *yad-bhavishya*.

† The city of victory. A common name of places.

‡ Ambassador of the sea.

§ Gem-splendour.

woman, although in our arms, is altogether to be suspected. What satisfaction then can there be in the sacred law, in princes, or in women?'

One day it so fell out, that being seen by her husband kissing one of the young men of the house, she ran instantly towards him and cried,—My dear, this servant must be exceedingly distressed for food, for he has been eating some camphire which I had brought home for thy use; and even now I have smelt to him, and find his breath scented with it!

It is truly said,

'What women eat is twofold; their cunning four-fold,' &c.

The servant, upon hearing the woman accuse him thus, appeared to be offended, and exclaimed,—What man can stay in a place with such a mistress as this, who is every minute smelling the servants' mouths? Saying which he went away; but his master sent for him back, and, with some difficulty, pacified him, and induced him to stay. I say, therefore, "He is a wise man," &c. To this What-will-be replied,—That is not to be which is not to be, &c.

Early in the morning Wit-against-it-when-come, being caught in a net, feigned himself dead, and remained quiet; but he was no sooner thrown out of the net, than he sprang into deep water, and thus made his escape; whilst What-will-be was taken by the fishermen, and so lost his life. I repeat, therefore, "These two, Fate-not-come," &c.

Then, concluded the tortoise, let it be contrived how I am to get to another lake. Where, demanded the two geese, will be the advantage of thy going to another place? Pray, replied the tortoise, only contrive the means, and I will go through the air along with you. How, said the geese, are we to contrive the means? Why, observed the tortoise, you must get a piece of wood, and take each of you one end of it in your beaks, from which I can suspend myself by my mouth, whilst you carry me along by the force of your wings. This contrivance will thus do, replied the geese; but,

One who is wise, in contriving the means, should consider the consequence. Some foolish boobies' young ones were devoured by a weasel before their faces.*

How did that happen? demanded the tortoise; and one of the geese related as follows:

FABLE V.

IN the north there is a mountain called Gridhrakootta, near which, on the banks of the Reva,† there

* In the original, *nakoola* (in Hindostanee, *nawl* or *noul*). A sagacious little animal, not bigger than a rat, noted for attacking and killing the most venomous serpents, after which it always runs into the thick grass, as it is supposed, in search of an antidote.

† Perhaps the proper name of the river we call the Rauvee which runs into the Indus.

used to be many boobies in a certain tree; and at the foot of the same tree a serpent lived in his hole, who used to devour the young boobies. An old bird hearing the lamentations of the afflicted boobies for the loss of their little ones, addressed them in these words: You should do thus:—Get some fish, and draw them along upon the ground from the hole of a weasel, as far as the serpent's hole, where you will leave them. Presently, the weasels, attracted by the scent of food, will go to the serpent's hole, and thus he is certainly to be discovered, and, from there being a natural enmity between them, thus to be destroyed. The plan was accordingly executed, and the serpent was discovered and eaten by the weasels, as they were hunting about the hollows of the tree for the fish; but soon after, the cries of the young boobies being heard by them, they mounted the tree and devoured them also. We repeat, therefore, said the two geese, "One who is wise, in contriving the means," &c. The people seeing us carrying thee along will cry out,—What a curious sight! Upon hearing which, if thou makest any reply, thou wilt certainly lose thy life; wherefore, upon all accounts, it is best to stay where we are. I will not speak a word, said the tortoise; what, do you take me for a fool?

In the manner described, at length the geese took up the tortoise, and flew away with him, hanging to the piece of wood; and presently, being discovered in that situation by some cowkeepers in the fields, they pursued them, crying out,—When he falls down, we will dress him and eat him upon the spot. No, said one of them, let us carry him home! Upon hearing which, the tortoise fell into a passion, to think how they intended to dispose of him; and whilst he opened his mouth to say,—You shall eat dust first! down he dropped, and was presently put an end to by those herdsmen. I therefore repeat, "He who doth not pay a due regard to the advice," &c., concluded the minister.

'We should always guard our speech; for from speaking ruin often ensueth; as in the downfall of the tortoise, who was being carried along by two geese.'

The booby, who had formerly been sent as a spy, having returned, addressed the royal goose in these words:—Please your Highness, at the very beginning I represented that it was necessary instantly to clear the castle; but that not having been done, this is the fruit of your neglect; and I have learnt that the burning of the castle was effected by the crow Cloud-colour, who had been employed for that purpose by the enemy's minister the vulture. The king, sighing, said,

'He who placeth confidence in an enemy, either from inclination or necessity, awaketh from his delusion, like one who hath fallen from the top of a tree in his sleep!'

And when Cloud-colour, continued the spy, had effected the burning of the castle, he went to king Chitra-varna; who being well satisfied with what he had done, said,—Let this Cloud-colour be appointed governor of Karpura-dweepa; for, it is said,

'One should not forget the labours of a servant who hath performed his duty; but should encourage him with rewards, with our hearts, with our speech, and with our eyes,'

Then the vulture, who is the prime minister, continued the spy, said,—Please your Highness, let some station be given to him inferior to that of the principal one; for,

'How is it possible to punish one who hath been raised to a superior station? The assistance, O king, which is rendered to those of low degree, is like endeavouring to please bears.'

A low person should never be placed in the station of the great.

One of low degree having obtained a worthy station, seeketh to destroy his master; like the mouse, who, having been raised to the state of a tiger, went to kill the hermit.

How was that? said the peacock king; and the minister related the following story:

FABLE VI.

In a forest of the prophet Gowtama,* which is dedicated to acts of penitential mortifications, there was a hermit, whose name was Maha-tapa. One day seeing a young mouse fall from the mouth of a crow near his hermitage, out of compassion he took it up, and reared it with broken particles of rice. He now observed that the cat was seeking to destroy it; so, by the sacred powers of a saint, he metamorphosed his mouse into a cat; but his cat being afraid of his dog, he changed her into a dog; and the dog being terrified at the tiger, at length he was transformed into a tiger. The holy man now regarded the tiger as no ways superior to his mouse. But the people who came to visit the hermit, used to tell one another that the tiger which they saw there had been made so by the power of the saint, from a mouse; and this being overheard by the tiger, he was very uneasy, and said to himself,—As long as this hermit is alive, the disgraceful story of my former state will be brought

* The declared author of a metaphysical work in the Sanskrit language, called Nyaya-darsana, the first volume of which is said to have been deposited in the British Museum.

to my ears; saying which, he went to kill his protector; but as the holy man penetrated his design with his supernatural eye, he reduced him to his former state of a mouse. I repeat, therefore, "One of low degree," &c. Please to attend to this also, said the minister:

A certain booby after having devoured fish of every size and quality, at length is killed from his attempting a crab out of mere gluttony.

How was that? demanded Chitra-varna; and his minister related the following story:

FABLE VII.

In the country of Malava there is a lake distinguished by the name of Padma-garbha, where lived an old booby, who, being deprived of his former abilities, stood and feigned to appear like one who was troubled in mind; in which situation being observed by a crab at a distance, the latter asked him why he stood there, and did not look for food. You know, replied the booby, that fish is what I live upon; and I know for certain that fishermen are coming to catch them all; for, as I was looking about the skirts of the next village, I overheard the conversation of some watermen upon that subject; so this being the case, I have lost my appetite with reflecting that, when our food is gone, death will soon follow. This being overheard by all the fish, they observed to one another that it was proper to look out for assistance whilst they had time; and, said they, let us ask the booby himself what is best to be done; for,

'One may better form a connection with an enemy who will render one assistance, than with a friend who would do one an injury. These two should rather be distinguished according to the good or injury they do to one.'

Accordingly, the fish accosted the booby, and said,—Pray, master booby, tell us what means can be devised for our safety upon this occasion? There is one way to be safe, replied the artful booby, and that is, going to another pond, whither I am willing to transport you. The fish, in the greatness of their fears, consented to this proposal, and their treacherous deliverer devoured them all one by one as he took them out of the water. At length, the crab asked him to take him also; and the booby, although he had never before had any inclination to taste one of his species, took him up with great marks of respect, and carried him ashore; when the crab seeing the ground covered with the bones of the fish which the booby had destroyed, cried to herself,—Alas, how unfortunate! I shall certainly be killed too, unless I can contrive some means of escaping. Let me try immediately what the occasion requires. They say,

'In times of danger it is proper to be alarmed until danger be near at hand; but when we perceive that danger is near, one should oppose it as if one were not afraid.

'When one attacked beholdeth no safety for himself, if he be a wise man, he will die fighting with his foe.'

It is also said, that

"As out of battle death is certain," &c.

The crab having come to this resolution, he seized the opportunity, when the booby stretched out his neck to devour him, to tear open his throat with the pincers of his claws. Wherefore I repeat, "A certain booby," &c.

Attend, said the peacock king, to what I have been thinking of:—That if Cloud-colour be left governor here, all the choice things which Karpura-dweepa produces may be sent to us to enjoy in great luxury, when we shall be returned to the Vindhya mountains. The minister, laughing at the king's proposal, replied,—Please your Highness,

He who rejoiceth over an unaccomplished design, may meet with disgrace; like the Brahman who brake the pots and pans.

How did that happen? demanded the king; and the minister related the following story:

FABLE VIII.

In the city of Devee-kotta* there was a Brahman whose name was Deva-Sarma.† One lucky evening he found a curious dish,‡ which he took with him into a potter's warehouse full of earthenware, and throwing himself upon a bed which happened to be there,§ it being night, he began to express his thoughts upon the occasion in this manner:—If I dispose of this dish, I shall get ten Kapardakas‖ for it; and with that sum I may purchase many pots and pans, the sale of which will increase my capital so much, that I shall be able to lay in a large stock of cloth and the like; which having disposed of at a great advance, I shall have accumulated a fortune of a *lac* ¶ of money. With this I will marry four wives; and of these I will amuse myself with her who may prove the handsomest. This will create jealousy; so when the rival wives shall be quarrelling, then will I, overwhelmed with anger, hurl my stick at them, thus! Saying which, he flung his walking-stick out of his

* The city of the goddess. Its situation is forgotten.

† The peace of God.

‡ In the original, Saktubhuk-sarava, *a dish to eat tarts.*

§ It is very common to see a small bedstead in the shops in India.

‖ Ten cowries.

¶ In Sanskrit, *laksha.* One hundred thousand (rupees).

hand with such force, that he not only brake his curious dish, but destroyed many of the pots and pans in the shop; the master of which hearing the noise, came in, and discovering the cause, disgraced the Brahman, and turned him out of doors.* I have said, therefore, concluded the minister, "He who rejoiceth," &c.

At the conclusion of this story the king took the vulture aside, and desired him to point out what he ought to do; and the minister replied,

'The conductors of princes intoxicated with power, as well as of wounded or restive elephants, get nothing but disgrace!'

Please your Highness, continued he, the castle hath been destroyed by us in the pride of strength; or rather, was it not by a stratagem dictated by your own glory? No, replied the king, it was thy own scheme. If my advice were to be followed, said the minister, we should now return to our own country; for upon the return of the rainy season, should we have to fight the enemy again, with an equal force, in their own country, we shall find it extremely difficult to retreat home if we should have occasion. Then, for the sake of peace and glory, treat with the enemy, and let us depart. We have taken their castle, and gained renown. This is the extent of my opinion.

* According to the original, *turned him out of the shop.*

'He is the companion of a prince, who, placing his duty before him, payeth no regard to his master's likings or dislikings, and tells him unwelcome truths.

'When victory in the battle is doubtful, one should wish to treat, even with an equal. One should not hesitate; for thus Vrihaspati hath declared.

'Who, except a child, would place his friends, his army, his kingdom, himself, and his reputation, in the doubtful balance of a battle?'

Besides,

Sometimes the overthrow of both happeneth; for were not Sunda and Upasunda, two giants of equal strength, killed by one another?

How was that? said the king; and the vulture related the following story:

FABLE IX.

IN former times there were two giants, the one called Sunda, and the other Upasunda, who wishing to conquer the three regions of the universe by the great exertions of their bodies, for a long time petitioned the deity with the crescent on his head to be propitious to their design. The god, pleased with their prayers, told them to ask a boon; but as the goddess Saraswatee* had the control of these two of dreadful

* The goddess of speech, harmony, and the arts.

forms, both their original wish and design were changed, and at length they said,—If the disposer of fortune be pleased with our prayers, give us, O Supreme Being, Parvatee thy own consort! Accordingly, the deity, although displeased at the request, from the absolute necessity of granting boons and from a kind of infatuation,* gave them Parvatee.

Having obtained her, they were presently inflamed by the beauty of her person, and eager for the ruin of the mother of the universe;† for they were involved in the darkness of sin. But as they were jealous of one another, they resolved to call upon some man of authority to determine which she should belong to; and instantly the deity, her lord, stood before them under the disguise of a venerable Brahman. We have obtained this female, said they, as a boon, and wish thee to determine which of us she should belong to. The Brahman replied,

'A Brahman is respectable because he is of a tribe the first in rank, a Kshatriya‡ for strength, and a Visya§ if he be possessed of wealth and grain.'

Now, seeing you two are of the second, or military order, your duty is fighting. These words made a due impression upon their minds; they fell upon

* In the original, *moorhata*, the state of being foolish.

† An epithet of the goddess Parvatee.

‡ The second of the four grand tribes; a soldier.

§ One of the third order in society; a merchant,

each other, but as they were equal in strength and courage, they died at the same instant from the blows they received from each other. I say, therefore, one should be inclined to treat even with one of equal force, concluded the vulture. Hast thou not told me this before? said the king. What, said the minister, did your Highness then comprehend the full extent of what I said? According to my opinion, this is not a proper time for the renewal of hostilities. King Hiranya-garbha is endued with those qualities which render him a proper person to treat with, and not to quarrel with. They say,

'There are seven descriptions with which it is deemed proper to form an alliance: men of veracity; men of family; men of justice and virtue; men of low degree, sometimes; such as are heads of a great fraternity; such as are powerful; and those who have been successful in many battles.

'He who formeth a connection with an honest man, from his love of truth, will not suffer thereby. And the man of family, it is very certain, will not be guilty of an unworthy action, even in the defence of life.

'To the strictly just and virtuous person, everything is annexed. The virtuous man, from his justice and the affection he hath for mankind, is the dispeller of sorrow and pain.

'It is expedient to form connections even with one of low degree, upon the approach of our own destruction, and when, without his protection, a worthy person might be ruined.

'He who is the head of a confederacy of brothers, from their compactness, is as difficult to be rooted out as a bamboo* surrounded by impenetrable thorns.

'There is no ordinance for our contending with the strong: the clouds never pass against the wind.

'From the glory of him who hath been victorious in many battles, as from the glory of the son of Jarnadagnee,† all, at all times, and everywhere, is enjoyed.

'Seeing he who hath been victorious in many battles meeteth not death, his enemies are captivated by his glory.'

Then I repeat, that the royal goose, being endued with many of these qualities, is worthy to be treated with. The minister now orders the booby to go to the enemy's camp, and to return with what further intelligence he could pick up.

I now wish thee, said the peacock king, to inform me how many there are with whom it may be im-

* In Sanskrit, *vangsa*. They grow in clumps, and often so closely connected by their own knotted branches, that it is with great difficulty they can be separated.

† The father of that Ram who is said to have destroyed, in several battles, all the males of the military order.

proper to enter into an alliance; and the vulture minister replied,—I am about to tell your Highness, repeating the following verses:

'The young, the old, the long afflicted, and such as have been excommunicated by their tribe; the fearful, and those whose followers are timid; the covetous, and those whose followers are covetous;

'Those whose principal officers are void of attachment, he who possesseth too much power in affairs, one who in his counsels is of many opinions, and he who speaketh disrespectfully of the gods or the Brahmans;

'He who is naturally unfortunate, and he who is always consulting fate; one afflicted with famine and pestilence, and he who possesseth a disorderly army;

'One who doth not stay in his own country, one who is beset with many enemies, he who hath an army out of time,* and one who hath departed from the true religion: these make twenty descriptions of persons,

'With whom it is not proper to enter into alliance, and whom one should do nothing but check; for if such as these go to war, they presently fall into the power of their enemies.

'If he be a child, his people are not ready to fight,

* Out of season, or when there is no occasion for an army.

because of the insignificance of his nature, and the inability of an infant to pay the reward or punish, for fighting or not fighting

'Be he one oppressed with age, or with some tedious infirmity, deprived of the power of exertion, he is inevitably overcome of himself.

'He who hath been expelled by all his kindred is easily to be defeated; for his relations too, out of respect for themselves, are ready to destroy him.

'Be he a coward, he himself will flee to avoid the battle; and if his troops are dastards, they will forsake him in the field.

'The followers of the covetous refuse to fight, because there is no distribution of the spoils; and where the attendants are so, they mutiny for pay, and murder their leaders.

'If the principal officers are not attached, their chief is forsaken by them in the midst of the battle; and if he be one who hath too much power in affairs, he expecteth superior attention.

'He who in his counsels is of many minds, is hateful to his ministers; and because of the unsteadiness of his mind, he is neglected by them in his necessary affairs.

'As religion is always most powerful, so he who despiseth the gods or a Brahman, of himself goeth to naught; and so doth he who is smitten by fate.

'Those who first study fate, and say,—Fate is the

only cause of fortune and misfortune, terrify themselves.

'He who is surrounded by famine and pestilence, of himself yieldeth; and he who hath a disorderly army, hath no power to fight.

'One who is out of his own country is defeated by a very trifling enemy: the smallest alligator in his own element gripeth the largest elephant.

'He who hath many enemies is like a pigeon among kites: whatever way he turneth, he is encountered by misfortune.

'If he be one who marcheth his army out of season, he is destroyed by fighting against the weather. He will suffer like the crow, who, venturing out at midnight, had his eyes picked out by an owl.

'One should, on no account, enter into any connection with one who hath departed from the faith; for, although he be bound by treaty, he will, because of his own unrighteousness, break his engagement.'

In addition to all this, continued the minister, I shall remind your Highness of the following particulars: Uniting, disputing, halting, marching, surrendering, separating, are denominated the "six modes."* For the commencement of an expedition the necessaries are, men, stores, treasure, time, and place; the possession of which is proper, as a pro-

* In the original, *shadgoona*.

tection against misfortune, as well as for the accomplishment of a design: they are called "the secret of five members."* Pacifying, giving, dividing, punishing, are distinguished by the appellation of "the four means."† Resolution, authority, good counsel, are denoted "the three powers."‡ Those sovereigns who attend to all these things are always victorious; for, they say,

'The success which is to be acquired by those who are acquainted with the rules of policy and prudence, is not to be gained by the price of abandoning life; for such knowledge causeth irresolution to fly from the body.

'He is always possessed of riches, whose followers are well attached, whose spies are concealed, and whose counsels are kept private; and he who doth not speak with unkindness to his fellow-creatures, may govern the whole world to the extremities of the ocean.'

But please your Highness, continued the minister, although peace has been proposed by that great statesman the vulture, still his master will not consent to it, because of his recent success. Then let this be done: The king of Singhala-dweepa,§ the Sarasà

* Panchango-mantra.

† Of concluding a war, is understood. In Sanskrit, Chatwara-upaya.

‡ Traya-sakti.

§ Ceylon.

Mahabala* is our friend; let him raise a disturbance in Jambu-dweepa, the enemy's country.

'A wise man having practised great secrecy, marching with a well-composed army, may alarm an opponent; and he who is alarmed will make peace with him with whom he hath been at variance.'†

The royal goose having consented to this proposal, one Vichitra a booby was dispatched to Singhala-dweepa with a very private letter.‡

In the meantime the spy returning from the peacock's camp, said,—Please your Highness, attend to what I have to inform you of. The vulture minister said to the peacock king,—Although Cloud-colour the crow was so long in the enemy's castle, what if he doth or doth not know whether the royal goose, Hiranya-garbha, be possessed of those qualities which are necessary towards our treating with him? After this, continued the spy, the peacock king having called Cloud-colour before him, asked him what sort of a character that same royal goose, Hiranya-garbha, was, and what sort of minister he had. To this the crow replied,—Please your Highness, Hiranya-garbha is as noble as king Yudhi-

* Great-strength.

† There is such a play upon words in the original of this verse, that the translation is but a faint resemblance.

‡ The original expression seems to favour the idea of their being acquainted with the art of writing in cypher.

shtira,* and a person of great sincerity; and as to his master, his likeness is nowhere to be discovered. If he be as thou hast described him, observed the king, how was it that he was deceived by thee?

The crow replied,

'What great ingenuity is there in deceiving him whose confidence one hath gained? Is the term manhood his who mounteth upon the bed, and destroyeth those that are asleep?'

Attend, please your Highness,—I was discovered by the minister from the beginning; but the king his master, being himself one in whom the greatest confidence may be placed, was easily imposed upon by me; according to the following saying:

He who, judging by what passeth in his own breast, believeth a knave to be a person of veracity, is deceived; as the Brahman was concerning his goat.

Pray how was that? demanded the king; and the spy told the following story:

FABLE X.

In the forest of the prophet Gowtama a certain Brahman, having determined to make an offering, went to a neighbouring village and purchased a

* Firm in battle. The name of a king who reigned over Hindostan upwards of four thousand years ago.

goat,* which having thrown across his shoulder, he turned towards home. As he was travelling along, he was perceived by three thieves. If, said they, we could by some artifice get the goat from that man, it would be a great proof of our address. Saying this, they agreed upon their stratagem, and executed it in this manner: They stationed themselves before the Brahman, and sat down under the trees in the road which led to his habitation, till he should come up to them. Soon after, he was accosted by one of them in this manner :—Is not that a dog? Brahman, what is the reason thou carriest it upon thy shoulder? The Brahman replied,—No, it is not a dog; it is a goat, which I have purchased to make an offering of. About a mile further on he met another of them, who repeating the same question, he took the goat from his shoulder, and putting it upon the ground, examined it again and again; and at length, replacing it upon his shoulder, he went on, quite staggered as it were.

The minds even of good men are staggered by the arguments of the wicked; but those who place confidence in them may suffer by it; like the camel Chitra-varna.

The king asked how that was; and the spy told him the following story:

* In the English translation of the fables falsely attributed to Pilpay, p. 206, it is a fine fat sheep; which, by-the-by, is an animal never sacrificed by the Hindoos.

FABLE XI.

IN a certain forest there was a lion whose name was Madotkatta,* and he had three attendants; a crow, a tiger, and a jackal. One day, as these three were roaming about, they met with a camel. They asked him whence he came, and whither he was travelling; and after he had given an account of himself, they introduced him to the lion; who, having given him assurances of protection, and determined that he should be called Chitra-varna, retained him in his service. Some time after, when the lion was out of order, his attendants were exceedingly at a loss for provisions, because for some time it had rained violently. So the crow, the tiger, and the jackal, agreed amongst themselves to contrive some way for the lion to kill the camel; for, said they, what is that thorn-eater † to us? Our master, observed the tiger, having given him assurances of safety, and taken him under his protection, then how can this be brought about? To which the crow replies,—At such a time as this, when our master's health is upon the decline for want of food, he will not scruple to commit a sin; for they say,

'A mother, when oppressed with hunger, will

* From *mada*, courage, vigour, mettle, and *ootkatta*, fierce.

† Camels are fond of browsing upon thorny plants,

abandon her own offspring; a female serpent, when distressed for food, will devour her own eggs. What crimes will they not commit who are pinched with hunger! Men pining for food become destitute of pity and compassion.

'Those who are intoxicated either with liquor or pleasure, the lazy, the passionate, the hungry, the covetous, the fearful, the hasty, and libertines, have no knowledge of justice.'

This being proved to the satisfaction of all parties, away they went to the lion; who, the moment he saw them, demanded if they had brought him anything to eat. The crow replied,—Sir, with all our endeavours, we have not been able to procure the smallest trifle. Then what means are there now left for my support? cried the lion. Sir, replied the crow, from your refusing the food which you have in your power, we are all like to perish. What is there here for me to eat? eagerly demanded the lion. The camel! replied the crow, whispering it in the lion's ear. The noble beast at this proposal, touching the ground, and then his two ears, in abhorrence, exclaimed,—Having, at our first interview, given him assurances of my protection, how can he now be treated thus? They say,

'Nor the gift of cattle, nor the gift of land, nor the gift of bread, nor the gift of milk, is to be compared with that which men call the greatest of all gifts: the gift of assurance from injury!'

Again:

'He who hath defended one who had claimed his protection, receiveth the full reward which is the fruit of an Aswa-medha sacrifice,* rendered more worthy by the addition of everything which is estimable!'

The crow replied,—Under these circumstances it is not proper that your Highness should put him to death; but suppose we so contrive, that he shall consent to offer his own body? The lion hearing this, remained silent; but the crow, finding an opportunity, made a pretence to carry all his friends and the camel before him; when he addressed him in this manner:—Please your Highness, as we can find nothing for you to eat, rather than my master shall fast, let him satisfy his hunger with all the flesh upon my poor body; for,

'When nature is forsaken by her lord, be she ever so great, she doth not survive. Although Dhanwantari be the physician, when life is departed, what can he do?

'All honours and endowments have their foundations in the sovereign; but although trees have their

* The sacrifice of the horse, in ancient times performed by a king at the conclusion of a great war in which he had been victorious.

roots, their being fruitful dependeth upon man's exertion.'

The lion nobly replied,—It is better to abandon life entirely, than to proceed in such an act as this! The jackal next offered himself; but the lion generously refusing, the tiger said, Live, O master, by my body! This never can be proper! said the noble beast; and, last of all, the camel, in whom was created the fullest confidence, offered himself as the rest had done; and instantly the tiger tore open his sides; and being thus cruelly murdered, he was devoured by them all. I say, therefore, "The minds even of good men," &c.

At length, said the spy, concluding the story of the three thieves, the Brahman having heard the third thief, like the former two, insist upon it, that he had a dog upon his shoulder, was convinced that it was a dog; and so, leaving his goat behind him, which the thieves presently took away and made a feast of, the good man washed himself* and went home. Whence, I say, "He who, judging by what passeth in his own breast," &c.

Cloud-colour, said the peacock king to the crow, thou wert a long time amongst the enemy,—pray how are their orders executed? Please your Highness, replied the crow, what is there not done by

* Because he had touched what he supposed a dog, which is esteemed an unclean animal.

servants who have their master's affairs at heart, or from a power derived from one's own necessities?

'Do not men, O king, bear burning wood upon their heads; and the force of rivers, simply by washing their roots, sweep trees away?'

When a wise man findeth an occasion, he may bear away his enemy upon his shoulder, as it were; just like the old serpent who killed the frogs.

How did that happen? said the peacock king; and the crow related the following story:

FABLE XII.

THERE was an old serpent, by name Manda-visarpa,* who, because of his great age, being unable to seek food for himself, threw himself down the bank of a pond, where he remained, till a certain frog seeing him at a distance, asked him what was the reason he did not hunt about for food? Leave me! cried the serpent, what occasion hast thou to inquire into the story of such an unfortunate wretch as I? The frog, who was not a little pleased to find his enemy in distress, desired him, by all means, to make him acquainted with the cause of his trouble. You must know, then, said the serpent, that here in the town of Brahma-pura, the son of one Kowndinya a Brahman,

* Slow-glide.

in the twentieth year of his age, and endued with every virtue and accomplishment, by the will of fate, was some time since bitten by cruel me! His father beholding his beloved son Shuseela, for that was his name, lying dead, fell mad for grief, and rolled himself upon the ground. In the meantime, the people of the city, his kindred, friends, and connections, all came and sat down upon the spot where he lay. They say,

'He is a friend who attendeth one at a feast, in affliction, in famine, in disputing with an enemy, at the king's gate,* and in the cemetery.' †

Amongst the rest, there was a certain pilgrim, whose name was Kapila, ‡ by whom the father of the youth was thus addressed,—Art thou deprived of reason, Kowndinya, that thou thus lamentest the dead? Hear me!

'Where are those sovereigns of the world, with all their numerous armies and splendid equipage, of whose departure the earth, even now, beareth testimony?

'In the body is concealed its decay, prosperity is

* Figuratively, when in confinement.

† The original word conveys the idea of a place by a river's side, where those whose lives are despaired of are carried and attended till dead, and where, at length, their bodies are burnt to ashes.

‡ The real name of one of their ancient saints, from whose works probably the following verses are quoted.

succeeded by adversity, and our meetings are soon followed by separations. Thus everything in nature is produced with that which will destroy it!

'Is not this body seen to waste, perceptibly, away? Is not its gradual consumption plainly to be discovered, as of water standing in a crude vessel?

'Youth and beauty, riches and stores of worldly goods, with the society of those we love, and even life itself, are all of short duration! Then let not the wise man therein be fascinated.

'As two planks floating on the surface of the mighty receptacle of the waters, meet, and having met, are separated for ever; so do beings in this life come together, and presently are parted.

'Upon the reduction of a body composed of five elements to those five principles, and each of those elements to its own womb, what cause is there for lamentation? *

'As many tender connections as the animal man formeth for himself, so many thorns of sorrow are there ingrafted in his heart.

'This is not a place for any one long to cohabit with another; nay, not even with his own body: then how can he expect it with another?

'The dissolution of a body foretelleth a new birth:

* The five elements mentioned in this verse are, fire, air, water, earth, and a subtile matter they call *akas*.

thus the coming of death, which is not to be passed over, is as the entrance into life.*

'The dissolution of the delightful connections we form with those we love, is as dreadful as the total change to those who are become incurably blind.

'But as brooks run on to join their rivers, and do not turn back; so the days and nights seize mortals' lives, and proceed eternally.

'The society of the good, which contributeth so much to the relish of happiness in this world, is joined in the yoke of troubles, because its end is separation.

'Hence it is that the wise avoid the acquaintance of good men; for there is no remedy for the mind afflicted with the sorrow of separation.

'Many noble and pious works were performed by Sagara and other ancient kings; but, alas! both they and their works are gone to decay.

'When he hath considered, and reconsidered, that severe punishment death, all the endeavours of the wit of man become as lax as skins of leather sprinkled by the rain!

'Every hero of the human race, from the first night of his residence in the womb, day by day approacheth death.'

Then pay no attention to this world, continued the

* Regeneration in the literal sense.

good pilgrim; for sorrow is a proof of ignorance. Observe,

'If separation be the cause, and ignorance be not the cause, how is it, that after days have passed away, sorrow is changed into childishness?'

Wherefore, compose thy troubled mind, and dispel all thought of grief; for they say,

'Not to think is the grand remedy, when our children are untimely born,* and against those weapons of deep sorrow, which penetrate the heart.'

The afflicted Kowndinya, roused by these words, got up as it were from a trance, and cried,—Since it be so, enough of dwelling in the hell of houses! I will presently retire into the wilderness! † Hold, my son, replied the benevolent Kapila.

'Those who yield to their passions will experience evils, even in the wilderness. To restrain the five organs of perception, even in a house, is doing penance. The habitation of him whose passions are well regulated, and who proceedeth but in such actions as are irreproachable, is as the wilderness of penitence.'

* A Hindoo's hopes of happiness after death greatly depend upon his having children to perform the ceremonies of the Sradha (offering cakes to the manes of their ancestors), by which he is taught to expect his soul will be released from the torments of Naraka.

† It is very common, at this time, for men to quit their wives and families, and all worldly concerns, to lead a godly life in some retired place, or else to wander about the country as beggars.

For they say,

'The afflicted even should practise the duties of religion, whatever mode of life they may choose, and wherever their abode may be; and our conduct should be equal unto all beings; for distinctions are not authorized by religion.'

Again:

'Those who eat but to support life, who wed but for the sake of progeny, and who speak but to declare the truth, surmount difficulties.'

Again:

'Suppose thyself a river and a holy pilgrimage in the land of Bharata,* of which truth is the water, good actions the banks, and compassion the current;

* This word is a derivative from Bharata, one of their most ancient kings; and it is the only name formerly used by the natives themselves for the countries we include in the term India; for both the appellation Hindoo for the people, and Hindostan for the country, now generally used by natives and foreigners, were probably given them by their neighbours the Persians. The river improperly called the Indus is quite out of the question, either as giving a name to the country, as many have imagined, or borrowing one from it, according to the opinion of the late Alexander Dow, Esq., in the dissertation prefixed to his "History of Hindostan," p. 31, who in the same page asserts, that "the Hindoos are so called from Indoo or Hindoo, which in the Shanscrita language signifies the moon." It is true that *eendoo* is one of the names of the moon, but not *hindoo*. Let it suffice that there are no such words as Hindoo or Hindostan in the Sanskrit language. In Persian we find Hind for the country, and Hindoo for the people. The proper name of the river we call the Indus, as written in Sanskrit characters, is Seendhoo, which, by the vulgar, is pronounced Seendh.

and then, O son of Pandu,* wash thyself therein, for the inward soul is not to be purified by common water.'

And thou shouldst pay particular attention to this saying:

'There is ease for him who quitteth this world, which is totally destitute of good, and overwhelmed with birth, death, old age, sickness, and sorrow. Pain is a thing of certain existence, but not ease; whence it is observed that the term ease is applied as a sort of remedy for one in pain.' †

To all this, continued the serpent, the afflicted father only replied,—Even so it is! but presently after the poor Brahman, in the height of his sorrow, denounced this curse against me, the author of his trouble,—that henceforward I should be doomed to carry frogs about upon my back as a beast of burden! After that, another Brahman who happened to be by, observing that Kowndinya was greatly revived by the wholesome doctrines of the pilgrim, addressed him in these words:

'Society should be avoided with all the efforts of the mind; but if it be not in one's power to avoid it,

* The name of an ancient king.

† According to this doctrine, *ease* is only a relative affection in this life, though a positive one in the next.

acquaintance should be formed with the good alone, for the company of good men is the remedy.'

Again:

'The tender passion should be avoided with all the resistance of the mind; but if it be not possible to conquer it, it should be indulged towards a wife alone, for she is the proper remedy.'

Kowndinya having heard this, and being by the salutary counsel of Kapila quite cured of his affliction, took the staff according to the usual forms;* and poor I, concluded the serpent, lie here under the power of a Brahman's curse, ready to carry any frog that shall choose to mount upon my back!

The frog. who had been attentive to this long story, upon hearing the last words of the serpent, went away to inform the chief of the pool of it, who, soon after making his appearance, the serpent placed him upon his back and carried him about, keeping a gentle easy pace. The king of the frogs was so pleased with his ride, that he came again the next day; but upon finding the serpent unable to carry him, and asking him what was the cause of his weakness, the artful animal replied that he was totally deprived of his strength for want of food. Upon this

* He renounced the cares of the world to lead the life of a Brahmacharee (literally one who walketh in God). The ceremonies of taking the staff are fully explained in the laws of Manoo, chapter ii.

the frog ordered him to be fed, every day, with as many of his subjects as he might choose; and the serpent having, by degrees, eaten all the frogs which were to be found in the pond, at length devoured his benefactor. I repeat, therefore, said the crow, "When a wise man," &c.

Let us have done with the repetition of old stories, observed the minister. In my opinion, said he, Hiranya-garbha is worthy of our alliance, and therefore I advise that a treaty be formed with him. Sir, said the king, is this your opinion? He has been defeated by us, and therefore he is at liberty to remain where he is, provided he consent to be our vassal; otherwise I command him to be attacked! Just as the king said this, the parrot came in from Jambu-dweepa, and informed his master the peacock that the Sarasa, who was king of Singhala-dweepa,* had lately invaded his country, and was still there. What is it thou sayest? cried the king in great confusion. Art thou too repeating some old story? said he. Well done, minister Chakra-vaka! exclaimed the vulture, well done! Whilst the peacock in great anger cried,—Let him stay there till I come, and I will extirpate him with his whole generation! To which the minister Far-see, smiling, replied,

'There is no necessity for imitating an autumnal

* Ceylon.

cloud! The thunder of the heavens our chief displayeth, whether on some account, or on no account, is of equal inefficacy.'

They say,

'A king should not dispute with too many enemies at a time; for even the proud serpent is inevitably destroyed by large swarms of wasps.'

Are we then, sir, continued the minister, to march back without concluding a peace? If we do, said he, I think we may have occasion to repent.

He who falleth into the power of anger before he hath made himself acquainted with another's merits, may have cause to be sorry for it; like the foolish Brahman after he had killed his weasel.

How was that? demanded the king; and his minister Far-see related the following story:

FABLE XIII.

AT Ujjayinee there lived a Brahman whose name was Mahdhava. His wife having been lately brought to bed, left her husband in charge of the infant, whilst she went to perform her ablutions.* As soon as she was gone, the Brahman, recollecting that the king's

* Women are enjoined by the law to perform positive ablutions in the river, after childbirth, and at certain periods every month, before they can return to their husband's bed.

offerings to the manes of his ancestors were about to be made, and seeing other Brahmans going to attend them, was prompted by his natural avarice to reflect in this manner: If I don't go directly, said he, some one else, having heard of it, will go and take away my share of the good things. They say,

Time drinketh up the essence of every work which should be done, and is not done quickly, whether it be an act of receiving, or an act of giving away.'

But, continued he, I have no one to take care of the door, then what am I to do, unless, indeed, I place this my long-beloved weasel there, who is as dear to me as the child itself, and then venture to go? In short, he did so, and went his way to the king's feast. It happened that soon after the Brahman left the house, as the weasel was passing near the child, he saw a black serpent gliding towards it, which he killed, and partly devoured; and when he saw his master returning, the affectionate little animal ran to meet him, with his mouth and legs all covered with blood; and he rolled himself upon the ground at the Brahman's feet in a very extraordinary manner; but the good man seeing him in such a condition, and hastily concluding that he had murdered his child, without further inquiry put the poor weasel to death. In short, when the Brahman went towards his child, and found it alive and well, and, at the same time, discovered the mangled remains of the black serpent upon the floor near it, the proofs of his weasel's merit and fidelity were so evident, that he suffered the most bitter pangs of sorrow and remorse. I repeat therefore, continued the minister, "He who falleth into the power of anger," &c. They say,

'A man should avoid these six evils: Lust, anger, avarice, pleasure, pride, and rashness; for, free of these, he may be happy.'

The peacock king replied,—So, minister, this is thy determination, is it? They say,

'The best qualities for a minister are, justice, thorough investigation, wise determination, firmness, and secrecy.'

Sir, said the minister in reply,

'Rashness in any undertaking should not be permitted; for the want of due investigation is the foundation of the greatest misfortunes. That success which merit is deserving of, attendeth of itself upon him who acteth with due deliberation.'

Then, if what I say is worthy of attention, peace should be concluded; for,

'Although four means are mentioned for the accomplishment of the work, the result of the whole number is uniting in peace.'

But, said the king, how may that be presently effected? Please your Highness, replied the minister, it shall be brought about speedily. They say,

'A bad subject is like an earthen vessel, easily to be broken and hard to be united; and a good one like a vessel of gold, not easily to be broken and not difficult to be reunited.'*

Especially, continued the minister, as both the king and his minister are exceedingly well informed of things in general; for this I knew from the beginning, as well from the reports of the crow Cloud-colour as from a single review of their conduct.

'The virtue and conduct of an absent person are, on all occasions, to be estimated by his works; wherefore one should weigh the actions of those who are out of sight by the effect.'

Let us have done with these answers and replies, cried the king, and let that which is most preferable be pursued. At length the minister, agreeable to his own counsel, went forth and waited near the castle, whilst a messenger ran to the royal goose Hiranya-garbha, and informed him that the minister of the peacock king was coming to treat for peace; but the

* The original words rendered by *broken*, *united*, and *reunited*, being applicable both to the breaking and mending of a vessel, as well as to friendly union and dissolution, the spirit of the simile could not well be preserved.

former, still suspecting something, said to his own minister, Know-all,—This again must be some spy or other coming to impose upon us! Please your Highness, replied Know-all, laughing as he spoke, there is great room for suspicion, for this same noble person who is coming is one who can see a great way;* else suspicion, which is the proof of a weak mind, should never be indulged.

'A wary goose having been once deceived by an enemy, whilst sitting in a very thick shade, in a lake, looking after the lotus plant, no more regardeth the cooling flower which is distressed by the appearance of day, and afraid of the stars.† Thus it is with the people of this world; having been once deceived, they suspect deceit in truth itself!'

Then, continued the minister, let a present, consisting of jewels, rich dresses, and the like, the best we can afford, be provided for him as a compliment. This being done accordingly, the minister, Know-all, went out and received the vulture, Far-see, in front of the castle, with every mark of respect; and presently conducted him into the presence of the royal goose, where he was permitted to be seated in a chair of state. Great minister, said Know-all, addressing himself to the vulture, now dispose of these your

* Alluding to his name Far-see.

† A lotus, which spreads its blossoms only in the night.

dominions according to your wish! Even so! added the royal goose. So be it! replied the vulture; but, said he, at present much negotiation is unnecessary; for they say,

'One should receive the covetous with gifts, the proud with joined hands, and the like tokens of submission, the ignorant with passages of poetry, and the wise and learned with whatever is suitable to their character.'

Again:

'A friend should be received with sincerity, relations with respect, women with gifts and compliments, and others with whatever is proper.'

Then let peace be presently concluded, that the most illustrious king Chitra-varna may depart, added the vulture. Inform us, said the minister Know-all, how peace is to be made. How many species of connections and alliances are there? demanded the king. I am about to tell you, said the vulture, so please to attend:

'When a king hath been overcome by one stronger than himself, no further opposition should be made; and the unfortunate party should sue for peace with all possible expedition.

'Those who are acquainted with the nature of

forming connections and alliances, declare that there are sixteen species, thus denominated:

Kapala,	Adrishtta-nara,
Upahara,	Adishtta,
Santana,	Atma-dishtta,
Sang-gata,	Upagraha,
Upanyasa,	Parikraya,
Prateekara,	Uch-chinna,
Sang-yoga,	Parabhooshana,
Purushantara,	Skandopaneya.

'The Kapala union is understood to be that where the parties simply form a connection upon an equal footing. The Upahara is when there is a gift from one of the parties.

'The Santana union is conceived to be that in forming which one of the parties delivereth up his family as a preliminary. The Sang-gata alliance is declared to be that which is formed with worthy men upon the foundation of friendship,

'Which is not to be broken by any accidents, whose purposes are the same in prosperity and adversity, and the measure of whose duration is the length of life.

This Sang-gata union, because of its superior excellence, may be compared to gold; and by others, who are acquainted with the doctrine of forming connections, it is called "the golden union."

'The Upanyasa alliance is declared, by those who are acquainted with that mode of uniting, to be that which is concluded upon terms pointed out by one of the parties.

'The alliance which is formed upon this principle, "I have formerly rendered him assistance, he shall now do so to me," is denominated the Prateekara mode.

'This also is called Prateekara: "I will render him assistance, and he shall do the same to me." Such was the alliance formed between Rama and Sugreeva.*

'It having been made to appear, that an expedition hath but one object, and upon these grounds a treaty is entered upon with united authority, it is called Sang-yoga.

'The Purushantara is an alliance formed upon this principle,—"Let my purpose be effected by the prime of both our armies;" and in settling which there is a price fixed.

'The Adrishtta-nara is, when a treaty is formed on such a proposal as this:—"My purpose is to be effected by thee alone;" in which also there is a price fixed.

'When a treaty is formed upon one party's quitting

* The latter was a baboon who assisted the former in his wars against Ravana, the king of Ceylon.

his enemy for a fine of a portion of his lands, it is denominated Adishtta.

'The conjunction formed with one's own army * is called Atma-dishtta; and that for the preservation of life, is denominated Upagraha.

'When a moiety, or even the whole, of the treasure is surrendered to save the rest of the property, the treaty is styled Parikraya; and if the consideration be the most valuable part of the lands, the term is Uch-chinna.

When the purchase of peace is made with a gift of the whole of the fruits of the earth, it is called Parabhooshana; and, lastly, when by a gift of the fruits which have been gathered, willingly borne upon the shoulder, Skandhopaneya.

'There are also these four distinctions of alliance: "That of reciprocal assistance, that of friendship, that of relationship, and that which is purchased with a gift."

'It is the opinion of Guru,† that alliance and assistance mean the same. There are many modes of alliance by gifts; but these are all rejected by friendship.

'The conqueror, from his being the strongest, is not wont to retreat without having gained something;

* The nature of this compact is not easily to be ascertained, for the name given to it does not explain it.

† Vreehaspatee, the Guru or spiritual director of the good spirits.

whence no other mode than the Upahara is known to him.'

The minister Know-all replied,—Hear this!

'To say, "This is one of us, or this is a stranger," is the mode of estimating practised by trifling minds. To those of more generous principles, the whole world is but as one family!'

Again:

'He who regardeth another's wife as his mother, another's goods as clods of earth, and all mankind as himself, is a philosopher.'

You are a philosopher, said the royal goose to the vulture, and therefore I desire you will point out what is to be done in this affair. Your Highness is pleased to compliment, replied the minister Far-see. The poet says,

'What name shall we give to him who inhabiteth a body destitute of justice, when that body, to-day or to-morrow, is subject to death by the fever of sickness or sorrow?

'When we consider this world in the light of a thirsty deer in a moment to be destroyed, it is proper to form connections with good people, for the sake of virtue, and for the sake of happiness.'

Then, continued the vulture, the business should be settled according to this saying, which corresponds with my own opinion,

'Truth being weighed against a thousand Aswamedha sacrifices, was found to be of more consequence than the whole thousand offerings.'

Wherefore, let the name of Truth be the divine precedent for both and each of us; and let the alliance between us be that which is distinguished by the title of The Golden Union!

The minister Know-all having signified his approbation of the proposed terms, Far-see was complimented with a present of rich cloth and jewels; and being exceedingly rejoiced at the event of his negotiations, he took his leave of the royal goose, and returned with the minister Know-all into the presence of his own sovereign. The peacock king ratified the peace, and, at the instance of the vulture, entered into a conversation with Know-all, in which he paid him many compliments; at the conclusion of which the latter had leave to depart, and he presently repaired to the camp of the royal goose.

The minister Far-see now tells his master, that as their designs were happily accomplished, it was advisable to direct their march towards home, the mountains of Vindhya. His advice was followed, and the whole army arrived at their respective habitations to enjoy in peace those fruits their hearts most longed for.

Now declare, said Vishnu-Sarma to his royal pupils, what more I am to tell you! Through the great condescension of our reverend master, replied the young princes, being made acquainted with every thing which relates to the royal department of negotiation, we are satisfied. May this conclusion render you equally so! said Vishnu-Sarma, repeating these lines:

'May peace for ever yield happiness to all the victorious possessors of the earth! May just men be for ever free from adversity, and the fame of those who do good long flourish! May prudence, like a glorious sun, shine continually on your breasts! May the earth, with all her vast productions, long remain for your enjoyment!'

THE END.

A. Bonner, Printer, 1 & 2 Took's Court, London, E.C.

ROUTLEDGE'S POPULAR LIBRARY.

Large demy 8vo, cloth, each vol. **3/6.**

A collection of standard works, well printed and uniformly bound.

1 **Arabian Nights' Entertainment.** 750 pp., with 8 plates.

2 *CARLETON (W.).* **Traits and Stories of the Irish Peasantry.** 818 pp.

3 *DISRAELI (I.).* **Curiosities of Literature.** 598 pp., with a portrait.

4 **Don Quixote,** transl. by JARVIS. 544 pp., with 9 plates. CERVANTES

5 *EMERSON (R. W.).* **Works.** 640 pp., with a steel portrait.

6 *EURIPIDES.* **Plays,** transl. by R. POTTER. 894 pp.

7 *FERNANDEZ (J.).* **Reciter.** 512 pp., with a portrait.

8 **Gil Blas,** transl. by SMOLLETT. 456 pp., with plates by PINWELL. LESAGE

9 *GOLDSMITH (Oliver).* **Complete Works in Prose and Verse.** 736 pp.

10 *HOLMES (O. W.).* **Breakfast Table Series** (Autocrat, Poet, and Professor at the Breakfast Table). 615 pp., with an engraved portrait.

11 *HOMER.* **Iliad and Odyssey,** transl. by A. POPE; edited by H. F. CARY, M.A. 534 pp.

12 *LAMB (C.).* **Works;** complete, edit. by C. KENT. 706 pp.

13 *MACKAY (Dr. C.)* **1001 Gems of Prose.** 538 pp.

14 —— **Memoirs of Extraordinary Popular Delusions.** 638 pp., with 116 woodcuts.

15 *MAHONEY (F.).* **The Works of Father Prout.** 542 pp., with a portrait.

16 *MILL (J. S.).* **Principles of Political Economy.** 640 pp.

17 *MONTAIGNE (M. de).* **Essays,** transl. by FLORIO. 640 pp.

18 *SHAKESPEARE (W.).* **Works,** ed. by C. KNIGHT. 1092 pp.

19 *SMITH (A.).* **The Wealth of Nations.** 796 pp.

20 **Spectator (The).** 944 pp.

21 **The same.** Large type edn., edit. by Prof. H. MORLEY. 3 vols. 2208 pp.

22 *STERNE (L.).* **Complete Works.**

23 **Ten Thousand Wonderful Things.** 704 pp., with hundreds of illns. E. T. KING

HISTORICAL AND BIOGRAPHICAL SECTION.

23 *BOSWELL (J.).* **Life of Johnson.** 530 pp.

24 *CARLYLE (T).* **History of the French Revolution.** 240 pp., with an engraved portrait.

25 —— **Lives of Schiller and Sterling.** 428 pp.

26 *D'AUBIGNÉ (M.).* **Story of the Reformation.** 594 pp.

27 *DAVENPORT (R. A.)* **History of the Bastile and its Principal Captives, with a History of the Man in the Iron Mask.** 554 pp.

ROUTLEDGE'S POPULAR LIBRARY—*Continued.*

28 *DEFOE (D.)* **Journal of the Plague Year.** 440 pp., with 4 steel plates by G. CRUIKSHANK.

29 *FROISSART (Sir J).* **Chronicles of England, France, and Spain.** 512 pp., with 8 plates.

30 *HOWITT (W.).* **Homes and Haunts of British Poets.** 648 pp., with illns.

31 *JOSEPHUS.* **Works,** transl. by WHISTON. 768 pp.

32 *LEWES (G. H.).* **Biographical History of Philosophy.** 650 pp.

33 *MACAULAY (Lord).* **Essays; and Lays of Ancient Rome.** 924 pp., with an engraved portrait.

34 *MILMAN (Dean).* **History of the Jews.** 640 pp.

35 *MOTLEY (J. T).* **Rise of the Dutch Republic.** 942 pp., with an engraved portrait.

36 *PLUTARCH.* **Lives of the Greeks and Romans.** 768 pp.

37 *PRESCOTT (W. H.).* **Charles the Fifth.**

38 —— **Conquest of Mexico.**

39 —— **Conquest of Peru; Miscellanies.**

40 —— **Ferdinand and Isabella.**

41 —— **Philip the Second.**

42 *ROBERTSON (Dr.).* **Charles V.**; and *PRESCOTT*, **Charles V.** 708 pp.

43 *SMILES (S.).* **The Huguenots in France.**

REFERENCE SECTION.

44 *ADAMS (W. H. D.)* **Concordance to Shakespeare.** 500 pp.

45 *BARTLETT (J).* **Familiar Quotations.** 532 pp.

46 *CRABBE (G.).* **English Synonyms,** with copious Illustrations and Examples. 638 pp.

47 *CRUDEN (A.).* **Concordance to the Old and New Test.** Edited by Rev. S. C. CAREY. 528 pp.

48 **Family Doctor (The).** 770 pp., with 500 illns.

49 *GROCOTT (J. C.).* **Familiar Quotations.** New edn., with an Appendix containing American Authors. 704 pp.

50 *LEMPRIÈRE (J).* **Classical Dictionary** (Unabridged) 700 pp.

51 *RAMAGE (C. T.)* **Beautiful Thoughts from French and Italian Authors.**

52 —— **Beautiful Thoughts from German and Spanish Authors.** 576 pp.

53 —— **Beautiful Thoughts from Greek Authors.** 605 pp.

54 —— **Beautiful Thoughts from Latin Authors.** 860 pp.

55 *WALKER (J).* **Rhyming Dictionary of the English Language.** 800 pp.

GEORGE ROUTLEDGE & SONS, LIMITED, LONDON.

14 *KEATS (J.).* **Poetical Works,** edit. by W. B. SCOTT. 382 pp., with portrait and plates.

15 *LONGFELLOW (H. W.).* **Poetical Works.** Complete copyright edn. 710 pp., with an engraved portrait.

16 *LOWELL (J. R.).* **Poetical Works.** 512 pp.

17 *MACKAY (Dr. C.; ed.)* **1001 Gems of English Poetry.** 23rd edn. 638 pp., with illns. by SIR J. MILLAIS, etc.

18 *MILTON (J.).* **Poetical Works;** illustr. by WM. HARVEY. 448 pp.

19 *MOORE (T.).* **Poetical Works.** Edited by CHARLES KENT. 640 pp.

20 *SCHILLER (F. v.).* **Plays and Poems;** with a portrait.

21 *SCOTT (Sir W.).* **Poetical and Dramatic Works;** with a Memoir by W. BELL SCOTT. 640 pp., with a portrait and illns.

22 *SHAKESPEARE (W.).* **Works.** Edit. by C. KNIGHT. 1092 pp.

23 —— **Works,** edit. by C. KNIGHT, Large-type edn. 3 vols., 2410 pp., with 3 collotype portraits.

24 *SHELLEY (P. B.).* **Poetical Works;** with a Memoir by W. BELL SCOTT. 634 pp., with illns.

25 *SOUTHEY (R.).* **Poetical Works.** 622 pp., with plates.

26 *SPENSER (E.).* **The Faerie Queene;** with the Epithalamium and a Glossary. 832 pp., with an engraved portrait.

27 *TENNYSON (Lord).* **Poetical Works.** 622 pp.

28 *WHITTIER (J. G.).* **Poetical Works.** 512 pp., with a portrait.

29 *WILLIS (N. P.).* **Poetical Works;** with a Memoir. 320 pp., with 4 plates.

30 *WORDSWORTH (W.).* **Poetical Works.** 572 pp., with illns.

MORLEY'S UNIVERSAL LIBRARY—*Continued.*

31 **Fables and Proverbs from the Sanskrit.** 278 pp.

32 **Famous Pamphlets.** 316 pp. Ed. by H. MORLEY

33 *GOETHE.* **Faust.** Part I.; with MARLOWE's Dr. Faustus.

34 —— **Faust**, Part II. 288 pp.

35 *GOLDSMITH.* **Vicar of Wakefield, Plays, and Poems.** 256 pp.

36 *HARRINGTON.* **Commonwealth of Oceana.** 282 pp.

37 *HERRICK.* **Hesperides.** 320 pp.

38 *HOBBES (T.).* **Leviathan.** 320 pp.

39 *HOMER.* **Iliad**, transl. by CHAPMAN. 220 pp.

40 *HOOKER.* **Ecclesiastical Polity.** 288 pp.

41 **Ideal Commonwealths.** 284 pp.

[*JOHNSON (Dr.).* **Rasselas.** *See* VOLTAIRE, *infra.*]

42 *JONSON (Ben).* **Plays and Poems.** 320 pp.

43 *LAMB (C.).* **Essays of Elia.** 288 pp.

44 *LEWIS (M. G.)* **Tales of Terror and Wonder.** 284 pp.

45 *LOCKE (J.).* **On Civil Government.** 320 pp.

46 *MACHIAVELLI (N.).* **The Prince.** 320 pp.

[*MARLOWE.* **Dr. Faustus.** *See* GOETHE, *supra.*]

47 **Mediæval Tales.** 288 pp. Ed. by Prof. H. MORLEY.

48 **Miscellany (A).** 272 pp. Ed. by Prof. H. MORLEY.

49 *MOLIÈRE (J. B. de).* **Plays from.** By DRYDEN, WYCHERLEY, FIELDING, etc.

50 *PEELE (G.).* **Plays and Poems.** 288 pp.

51 *PRAED (W. M.).* **Essays.** 280 pp.

52 *RABELAIS (F.).* **Gargantua.** Books I.—II. 320 pp.

53 —— **The Same.** Books III.—V. 320 pp.

54 *SCHILLER (F. v.).* **Poems and Ballads**, transl. by LYTTON. 384 pp.

55 *SCOTT (Sir W.).* **Demonology and Witchcraft.** 320 pp.

56 *SHERIDAN (R. B.).* **Plays.** 320 pp.

57 *SOPHOCLES.* **Plays:** transl. by T. FRANCKLIN. 320 pp.

58 *SOUTHEY (R.).* **Life of Nelson.** 282 pp.

59 *STERNE (L.)* **Tristram Shandy.** 186 pp.

60 *VIRGIL.* **Works.** Transl. by DRYDEN. 320 pp.

61 *VOLTAIRE.* **Candide:** and JOHNSON'S **Rasselas.** 288 pp.

62 *WALKER (T.).* **The Original.** 316 pp.

63 *WALTON (I.)* **Lives of Donne, Wotton, Hooker, and Herbert.** 284 pp.